LONDON

TRAVEL GUIDE

2023

The Complete London Tourist Guide and Information to make you Experience the city like a true local

By

Dallas J. Gresham

Copyright

LONDON TRAVEL GUIDE 2023:

The Complete London Tourist Guide and Information to make you Experience the city like a true local

By Dallas J. Gresham

The Complete London Tourist Guide and Information to make you Experience the city like a true local

INTRODUCTION TO LONDON

England's capital, London, is a fusion of many cultures, eras of history, and modernity. Being one of the most visited cities in the world, it provides both visitors and residents with a wide variety of experiences. In this dynamic metropolis, there is something for everyone, from the recognizable Big Ben and Tower of London to the busy neighborhoods of Camden and Soho. Monuments, museums, and old buildings in the city showcase its extensive past, while chic shops, eateries, and entertainment options showcase its contemporary culture. Whatever your interests—history, culture, or retail therapy—London has plenty to offer. Visit and discover the city that offers everything to suit every taste.

For centuries, London has been regarded as one of the world's most important cities. London has been instrumental in creating history and the modern world from the Roman invasion through the Industrial Revolution. Its busy streets and well-known sites, like Buckingham Palace and Westminster Abbey, reveal a city that has seen it all. But London is a city of invention and growth as well as history and tradition. London is a city that continuously pushes limits and sets new standards, from the cutting-edge technology of the Shard to the internationally famous museums and galleries. London is a city that never stops surprising and inspiring visitors with its multicultural population, top-notch entertainment, and limitless opportunities. Come and experience London's enchantment for yourself.

Going with a tour guide is very necessary when visiting London, and I'm here to assist you during your whole trip. From the finest locations to stay into the must-see attractions and secret jewels, I'll make sure you have an outstanding time in this vibrant city. Whether you are a seasoned tourist or a first-time visitor, I will customize your itinerary based on your interests and preferences. I will show you the finest of London, from the busy streets of Oxford Circus to the serene gardens of Hyde and Regent's Park, using my insider knowledge and local skills. I'll make sure you don't miss anything as I lead you through the city's rich history, culture, and art. Together, we will tour the city's busy streets, sample the delectable cuisine, find the secret treasures, and make lifelong memories. I'm here to make sure you make the most of your time in London, which is waiting for you.

A BRIEF OVERVIEW OF THE

CITY'S

HISTORY

AND

CULTURE

CHAPTER 1: A BRIEF OVERVIEW OF

THE CITY'S HISTORY AND CULTURE

Over 2,000 years of history have been devoted to London. Londinium was the initial name of the city when it was constructed by the Romans in AD 43. Roman engineers built a bridge across the Thames, establishing a crucial hub for communication and commerce. Many of the city's well-known structures, like St. Paul's Cathedral, were constructed during the Middle Ages when London rose to prominence as a hub of business and trade.

With the creation of opulent structures like the Globe Theatre and the founding of the Royal Society, London had a cultural and artistic rebirth throughout the Tudor and Elizabethan ages. The development of many of the city's renowned structures and the expansion of the city's infrastructure throughout the Georgian and Victorian periods contributed to the city's continuous growth and prosperity.

During World War II in the 20th century, London was brutally bombed, and most of the city was rebuilt in the years after the war. The diversified population, world-class museums and galleries, and thriving cultural scene make London a global metropolis today. The city is a hub for finance, commerce, and culture because of the presence of several significant multinational corporations and organizations.

London has always been a crossroads of cultures as well as a hub for growth and creativity. It is still one of the world's most significant and interesting cities today.

Speaking about history, London is home to several monuments and places that serve as reminders of the city's illustrious past. The Tower of London, a medieval castle that has served as a royal palace, prison, and treasury, Westminster Abbey, a Gothic cathedral that has witnessed numerous royal weddings and coronations, and St. Paul's Cathedral, a magnificent Baroque church created by Sir Christopher Wren, are some of the most well-known historical sites.

The National Gallery, which has one of the largest collections of European paintings, the British Museum, which houses one of the largest collections of historical artifacts in the world, and the Houses of Parliament, which is where the well-known Big Ben clock tower is located, are other noteworthy historical sites.

Along with these well-known attractions, the city is home to other lesser-known historical sites and undiscovered jewels. For instance, the Sir John Soane's Museum, a fascinating historical residence packed with art and relics, and the Old Spitalfields Market, an 18th-century market that has been turned into a hip destination for eating and shopping.

Numerous tourists are drawn to London in large part because of its history, and there are many chances to learn about and experience the city's fascinating past.

London is a multicultural metropolis with a population made up of individuals from all over the globe. The city's thriving cultural landscape, which features everything from top-notch museums and galleries to bustling street festivals and markets, reflects this variety.

A trip to London's West End, which is home to some of the most renowned theaters and musicals in the world, is one of the city's most recognizable cultural experiences. The magic of live theater may be enjoyed by visitors by attending a performance at one of the numerous theaters, such as the Globe Theatre or the London Palladium.

The British Museum, the National Gallery, and the Tate Modern are just a few of the top museums and art galleries in London. These museums give a fascinating look into the history and culture of London and other places by showcasing a broad variety of artwork and artifacts from across the globe.

The street art movement in the city is also booming, so it's typical to see vibrant murals and graffiti all over the place. Shoreditch, Brick Lane, and Camden are a few of the greatest areas to observe street art.

In addition to these cultural opportunities, London hosts a wide variety of festivals and events all year long. The London Jazz Celebration, which draws some of the best jazz performers in the world, and Notting Hill Carnival, the biggest street festival in Europe, are two of the most well-liked events.

London's culture is varied, vibrant, and always changing. In this vibrant city, there is something for everyone to enjoy, from the traditional to the modern.

Top things to do and see in London

With good reason, London is one of the most well-liked tourist destinations worldwide. The city offers a wide variety of activities and sights, from historical sites and cultural attractions to exciting nightlife and delectable food. The following are some of the best activities and sights in London:

1. **Visit Buckingham Palace:** As the monarch's official London home, Buckingham Palace is a popular tourist destination. During the summer, guests may explore the State Rooms or see the Changing of the Guard ritual.

One of the most recognizable buildings in the city is Buckingham Palace, which serves as the monarch's official home in London. It is situated in the center of London and is surrounded by well-kept parks and gardens. During the summer, guests visiting the palace may see the State Rooms or join in the Changing of the Guard event. Here is information on how to visit Buckingham Palace:

Timing: Tours usually take place from 9:30 a.m. to 7:30 p.m. from July through September, when the palace is available to guests. To minimize disappointment, it's essential to reserve your trip in advance since seats sometimes sell out rapidly.

The Changing of the Guard ceremony: This popular event is held every day at 11:30 a.m. and is well-attended by tourists. The ritual, which sees the Old Guard replaced by the New Guard, is an amazing sight.

The State Rooms: Throughout the summer, guests are welcome to enjoy a tour inside the monarch's official state residence, which is known as the State Rooms. The apartments' exquisite artwork, furniture, and antiques provide guests with a glimpse into the illustrious past and enduring traditions of the British monarchy.

The Buckingham Palace Garden: One of London's biggest private gardens, the palace garden is available to tourists in the summer. On a guided walk of the garden, guests may discover the many flora and trees there as well as the legacy and history of the palace.

The Queen's Gallery: The Queen's Gallery is a standalone structure within the grounds of the palace and is accessible to guests throughout the year. The exhibition presents artwork from the Royal Collection and offers a distinctive look into the British monarchy's past.

Dress Code: It is advised that visitors to the palace dress correctly and refrain from wearing shorts, skirts, or sleeveless shirts.

Transportation: Buckingham Palace is situated in the heart of London and is readily reached by public transportation. The palace is just a short walk from Victoria Station, the nearest subterranean station.

Anyone visiting London should pay a visit to Buckingham Palace, which offers a fascinating look into the illustrious past and enduring traditions of the British monarchy. There is something to attract everyone at Buckingham Royal, whether it is the Changing of the Guard ritual, the State Rooms, or the palace garden.

2. **Visit the Tower of London:** a medieval fortification that previously served as a jail and is now a museum displaying the Crown Jewels and the history of the monarchy.

Anyone interested in the history of England must visit The Tower of London, one of the city's most recognizable monuments. Throughout its history, the tower has functioned as a royal mint, a jail, a royal palace, and a site of execution. Today, it is a well-liked tourist destination. A guide to visiting the Tower of London is provided below:

Timing: The Tower of London is open daily from 9 a.m. to 5:30 p.m.; it's better to go early to beat the throng.

The Crown Jewels: The Crown Jewels, which are kept in the Jewel House, are one of the attractions in the Tower of London. One of the biggest and most expensive collections of its sort in the world, it comprises the crowns, scepters, and orbs that the English kings used.

The Yeoman Warders: The Yeoman Warders, sometimes referred to as Beefeaters, are a well-liked sight at the Tower of London. They operate as the tower's guardians and guides. Visitors may join a warder on a guided tour of the tower to learn about the tower's history and the responsibilities of the warders.

The Tower Bridge Exhibition: A well-liked attraction that offers tourists a distinctive viewpoint of the city is the Tower Bridge Exhibition. Visitors may traverse the bridge's glass floor and take in expansive views of London.

The White Tower: The White Tower, the Tower of London's oldest and most recognizable structure, is a must-see for anybody interested in the tower's history. The structure was utilized as a royal residence at first, then as a jail and an execution site.

The Royal Armouries: Located in the White Tower in the Tower of London, the Royal Armouries is the country's main repository for weapons and armor. Swords, helmets, and other armor and weaponry from many historical eras are on display for visitors to observe.

Transportation: The Tower of London is situated in the heart of the city and is readily reached by public transportation. The tower is a short distance from Tower Hill Station, which is the nearest subterranean station.

Anyone visiting London must pay a visit to the Tower of London, which offers a fascinating look into the history of England and the monarchy. There is something to intrigue everyone at the Tower of London, whether it is the Crown Jewels, the Yeoman Warders, or the White Tower.

3. **Explore the British Museum:** This well-known museum is home to a sizable collection of artwork and artifacts from all around the globe, including the Rosetta Stone and Parthenon sculptures.

Anyone interested in history and culture should visit the British Museum, one of the biggest and most well-known museums in the world. The museum holds a sizable collection of artifacts and works of art from all over the world and covers a broad variety of topics, including anthropology, archaeology, and the arts. The following is a guide to visiting the British Museum:

Timing: Admission to the museum is free, and it is open every day save Good Friday and Christmas Day. It's a good idea to schedule your visit in advance and to try to come early or late in the day to avoid crowds since the museum may be packed.

The Collection: The British Museum has an extensive and varied collection that contains artifacts from all over the globe as well as from several different cultures and historical eras. The Rosetta Stone, the Elgin Marbles, and the Egyptian mummies are a few of the most well-known items in the collection.

The Highlights Tour: If it's your first time visiting the museum, it's a good idea to take the Highlights Tour, which will expose you to some of the most well-known and significant pieces in the collection. A skilled guide conducts the tour, which usually lasts one hour.

The British Museum often holds temporary exhibits, which are a fantastic chance to gain more in-depth information about certain subjects or civilizations. Tickets for these exhibits may be bought in advance or on the day of the visit.

The Reading Room: The British Museum's Reading Room is one of the most renowned research libraries in the world and welcomes visitors by appointment. Anyone interested in research or academic study should pay a visit to the room, which is home to a sizable collection of books and manuscripts.

The Museum Shop: The Museum Shop of the British Museum offers a variety of goods, including books, jewelry, and home goods. It is a fantastic location to buy presents and souvenirs.

Getting There: The British Museum is situated in the Bloomsbury neighborhood of central London and is readily accessible by public transportation. Tottenham Court Road, the closest subway station, is just a short distance from the museum.

Anyone who is interested in history and culture should definitely pay a visit to the British Museum. Everyone can find something to enjoy at the British Museum, and whether you're a seasoned museum-goer or a first-time visitor, you'll undoubtedly leave with a better knowledge of the world's history and civilizations.

4. Go for a walk in Hyde Park: Hyde Park, one of London's biggest parks, is a well-liked spot to unwind and take in the city's greenery.

One of London's biggest and most well-known parks, Hyde Park is situated in the center of the city. On its 350 acres, the park is home to a number of attractions, including lakes, gardens, monuments, and museums. Here is some advice for going to Hyde Park:

Timing: Hyde Park is open every day of the week, all day long, and admission is free. When visitors may take advantage of the nicer weather and outdoor activities, the park is especially well-liked in the summer.

The Serpentine: A man-made lake in the middle of Hyde Park, The Serpentine is a well-liked destination for tourists looking to unwind and take in the view. Visitors may either rent a boat and explore the lake, or they can just sit by the water's edge and observe the passing boats.

The Hyde Park Speakers' Corner: This section in the park is set aside for anyone to get up and speak on whatever topic they want. Since the 19th century, the region has had a long history of serving as a venue for free speech and political protest.

The Hyde Park Winter Wonderland: Throughout the winter, Hyde Park is transformed into a winter wonderland, complete with a number of festive events including an ice rink, a Christmas market, and a giant wheel.

The Diana, Princess of Wales Memorial Fountain: This circular fountain, which can be seen in Hyde Park, was constructed in Princess Diana's honor. Children love to play in the water at the fountain, which is a popular area for tourists to unwind and take in the tranquil surroundings.

The Peter Pan Statue: The Peter Pan Statue is a bronze statue that can be seen in the Italian Garden and is a well-liked location for pictures. The monument, which portrays the well-known figure of Peter Pan, is a well-liked destination for families with young children.

The Serpentine Gallery: The Serpentine Gallery is a prominent gallery of modern art in London and is situated in Hyde Park. The gallery showcases a range of installations and exhibits by both well-known and up-and-coming artists.

Getting There: Hyde Park is situated in the heart of London and is readily reached by public transportation. The park is just a short walk from Hyde Park Corner, the nearest underground station.

Anyone visiting London should pay a visit to Hyde Park, which offers a window into the city's rich legacy and history. Everyone can find something to do in Hyde Park, whether they want to unwind by the Serpentine, see the monuments and museums, or participate in winter wonderland events.

5. <u>Visit the London Eye:</u> one of the city's most well-known tourist attractions, which gives sweeping views of the metropolis.

The South Bank of the River Thames in London, England is home to the enormous Ferris wheel known as the London Eye. It provides stunning views of the city and its attractions, including Buckingham Palace, the Houses of Parliament, and St. Paul's Cathedral, from its 135-meter (443-foot) height. Here is information on how to visit the London Eye:

Timing: Depending on the season, the London Eye's operation hours change every day. To organize your visit and prevent lengthy lineups, it is advised to consult the official website ahead of time.

Getting there: Public transit is a convenient means of getting to the London Eye, which is situated on the South Bank of the River Thames. Waterloo is the nearest underground station and is just a short distance from the wheel.

Available Tickets: The London Eye offers a variety of ticket types, including normal tickets, fast-track tickets, and VIP tickets. Depending on their financial situation and time limits, visitors may choose the ticket option that best meets their requirements.

The Experience: Each capsule on the London Eye provides panoramic views of the city and its landmarks, and the ride lasts for around 30 minutes. Through audio tours that are accessible in many different languages, visitors may learn about the history of London and its well-known monuments.

The London Eye 4D Experience: This option is available for those seeking an even more immersive experience. This includes a trip on the London Eye and a 4D movie that transports viewers across the city.

The London Eye River Boat: Tourists may combine their visit to the London Eye with a cruise down the River Thames, which offers a distinctive view of the city and its monuments.

Accessibility: Wheelchairs are available for use upon request, and the London Eye is completely accessible to those with impairments.

Anyone visiting London must see the London Eye, which offers a unique and spectacular view of the city. The London Eye has something for everyone, whether you're interested in the breathtaking vistas, the 4D experience, or the river cruise.

6. <u>Pay a visit to St. Paul's Cathedral:</u> which is a magnificent structure and one of the city's most recognizable attractions.

One of London's most well-known and recognizable buildings, St. Paul's Cathedral is recognized as one of the world's best examples of Baroque architecture. On Ludgate Hill in the center of the city, the cathedral has played a significant role in shaping London's skyline for more than three centuries. Here are several directions to St. Paul's Cathedral:

• **Hours:** Visitors are welcome in St. Paul's Cathedral every day save when it is being used for services. Normally open from 8:30 a.m. to 4:30 p.m., the cathedral keeps later hours in the summer.

• **The Dome:** The Dome, which gives panoramic views of the city from its observation galleries, is the highlight of every trip to St. Paul's Cathedral. For a distinctive view of London's skyline, visitors may ascend the Dome's 528 steps to the summit.

• **The Crypt:** The St. Paul's Cathedral's Crypt is the biggest in all of Europe and is home to many notable people's graves, including those of Admiral Lord Nelson and the Duke of Wellington. To learn about the history of the cathedral and its notable occupants, visitors may take a guided tour of the Crypt.

• **The Quire:** One of the most elaborately adorned areas of the cathedral, the Quire is where the choir performs. To understand more about the cathedral's history and design, visitors may join a guided tour of the Quire.

• **The Whispering Gallery:** This circular gallery, which sits just below the Dome, is renowned for its acoustics. From opposite ends of the gallery, visitors may whisper to one another and be heard as if they were standing right next to one another.

• **The Stone Gallery:** This path circles the base of the dome and offers views of the inside of the cathedral. To understand more about the cathedral's past and current design, guests may join a guided tour of the Stone Gallery.

• **Dress Code:** It is advised that visitors to St. Paul's Cathedral dress correctly and refrain from wearing shorts, skirts, or sleeveless shirts.

St. Paul's Cathedral is situated in the heart of London and is readily reached by public transportation. The cathedral is just a short walk from St. Paul's Station, which is the nearest subterranean station.

Anyone visiting London should pay a visit to St. Paul's Cathedral, which offers a fascinating look into the history and architecture of one of the city's most well-known buildings. There is something for everyone in St. Paul's Cathedral, whether you are interested in the Dome, the Crypt, or the Quire.

7. Take a stroll along the South Bank: This section of the River Thames is a dynamic center of culture, home to food carts, street performers, and famous sights like the London Dungeon and the National Theatre.

On the southern bank of the River Thames in London, there is a bustling and diverse neighborhood known as The South Bank. It is a well-liked tourist destination for both residents and visitors, and it is the location of many attractions, including galleries, theaters, museums, and street performers. Here is a map for exploring the South Bank on foot:

• **Begin with the London Eye:** This enormous Ferris wheel on the South Bank offers sweeping vistas of the city. You may either take a cab there or just stand there and take it all in from the beginning of your stroll.

• Take a stroll in the direction of the **SEA LIFE London Aquarium**, which is close to the London Eye and is home to over 600 kinds of aquatic life, including sharks, rays, and penguins.

• **Pay a visit to the National Theatre:** one of the top theaters in the nation, which is situated on the South Bank. Visitors have a choice of attending a concert or a guided tour of the venue.

• **Take a stroll through the Southbank Centre:** This cultural hub on the South Bank is home to a number of theaters, galleries, and performance venues. Visitors may take in a range of exhibits, performances, and activities or just unwind and take in the sights of the River Thames.

• **Visit the food market:** The South Bank is also home to a bustling food market that serves a variety of international cuisines, including street food, gourmet delicacies, and classic British fare.

• **Take a stroll along the river:** One of the nicest things about the South Bank is the chance to stroll along the river while admiring the cityscape. To experience the city from a new angle, you may either stroll along the river path or take a riverboat excursion.

• **Go to the Tate Modern:** One of the top museums for modern and contemporary art in the world, which is situated on the South Bank.

Visitors may explore a variety of exhibits and installations or just unwind in the museum's café while taking in the city views.

• **Finish your stroll at the Shakespeare's Globe:** Situated on the South Bank, the Shakespeare's Globe is a replica of the original theater where Shakespeare's plays were originally presented. Visitors have a choice of attending a concert or a guided tour of the venue.

Whether you're interested in art, culture, cuisine, or just taking in the city vistas, the South Bank is a dynamic and active location where there's always something going on. You will have a terrific time whether you decide to spend an hour or a whole day strolling around the South Bank.

8. Check out the Tate Modern: One of the biggest art museums in the world, which is built in a former power plant.

One of the biggest museums of its sort in the world, Tate Modern is a gallery of modern and contemporary art that is situated in London. Anyone interested in contemporary art must visit the gallery, which is located in a former power plant on the south bank of the River Thames. The Tate Modern visitation guide is as follows:

• **Exhibits:** Tate Modern hosts a variety of exhibitions throughout the year that include the creations of modern artists from all over the globe. A variety of artwork, including sculpture, photography, and multimedia installations, will be on display for visitors. To find out what exhibits are on show, it is essential to consult the Tate Modern website before going.

• **The Collection:** The Tate Modern collection includes more than 75,000 pieces of art that date from the early 20th century to the present. Visitors may expect to view works by some of the most well-known contemporary painters in the world, including Pablo Picasso, Henri Matisse, and Jackson Pollock, in the collection, which is scattered over multiple levels of the museum.

• **The Turbine Hall:** The Turbine Hall, one of Tate Modern's most recognizable elements, is a large, industrial area situated in the center of the museum. The hall often hosts large installations and exhibits, giving the artwork on a show a distinctive and dramatic setting.

• **Guided Tours:** Tate Modern provides a variety of guided tours, including audio tours, group tours, and tours suitable for families. These tours provide guests with a close-up view of the artwork on a show as well as insights into the artists' practices and the concepts that underlie their works.

• **The Terrace Bar:** Situated on the gallery's top level, The Terrace Bar provides breathtaking views of the River Thames and the city of London. Visitors may unwind while taking in the scenery by sipping a drink or eating something.

• **Accessibility:** Tate Modern is wheelchair-accessible and has elevator access to all gallery floors, as well as accessible restrooms and audio tours.

• **Transportation:** Public transportation is a convenient way to get to Tate Modern, which is situated on the south bank of the River Thames. The gallery is just a short distance from Southwark Underground Station, which is the closest one.

Anyone interested in contemporary art ought to make a trip to the Tate Modern. The gallery is a fascinating location that offers visitors an immersive and engaging experience thanks to its extensive collection of works by some of the most well-known contemporary artists in the world, as well as its distinctive Turbine Hall and breathtaking views over the River Thames.

9. Attend a performance in the West End: The theater district in London's West End is home to some of the finest plays, musicals, and operas in the world.

Some of the most renowned theaters and performances in the world are located in the West End, the center of London's theater area. Arts enthusiasts visiting London will discover a wide variety of performances to select from, including musicals, plays, operas, and ballets. Here are some tips for seeing a performance in the West End:

• **Picking a Show:** There are many different shows to pick from in the West End, making the decision difficult. Whether you're looking for a family-friendly performance, a modern play, or a classic musical, you may search for plays depending on your preferences.

Additionally, you may look up reviews and ratings online to aid in decision-making.

• **Purchasing Tickets:** It is advised to get tickets in advance since popular concerts may sell out very fast. Tickets may be purchased online or via a ticket broker. Be on the lookout for ticket fraud and make sure you only purchase tickets from reliable sources.

• **Timing:** Curtain timings for most West End performances range from 7 p.m. to 8 p.m. There are additional matinee performances on the weekends and sometimes throughout the week.

• **Dress Code:** Although there isn't one for West End performances, it's usually a good idea to wear something classy and comfortable.

• **Getting There:** The West End is conveniently placed in the heart of London and is accessible via public transportation. Charing Cross, Leicester Square, and Piccadilly Circus are the nearest subway stations to the theaters. To get to the theaters, you may either take a cab or walk, but be mindful of traffic and give yourself plenty of time.

• **Intermission Beverages and Food:** The majority of West End theaters offer a bar where patrons may purchase drinks and snacks. Be mindful that beverages might be pricey; if you want to save money, it's a good idea to bring your own.

• **Seating:** Stalls, circle, and balcony seats are among the choices available at West End theaters. When purchasing your tickets, you have the option of selecting your seat. To get a sense of the view you'll have, it's a good idea to look at the seating chart for the theater.

An unforgettable and memorable way to see London's rich cultural legacy is to attend a performance on the West End. The West End has something for every taste, whether you like plays, musicals, or the arts. It is a must-visit location for anybody traveling to London because of the huge range of performances and theaters it offers.

10. <u>Travel to Tower Bridge</u>: One of London's most distinctive structures, this bridge provides views of both the city and the river.

One of London's most recognizable sites and a must-see for tourists is Tower Bridge. The bridge, which lies on the River Thames, offers breathtaking views of the city and is a well-liked tourist destination. To visit the Tower Bridge, follow these instructions:

• **The Tower Bridge Exhibition:** Located within the bridge, the Tower Bridge Exhibition is a museum that educates visitors about the construction and history of the structure. The exhibition offers a chance to learn about the history and legacy of the bridge and includes interactive exhibits and displays.

• **The Glass Floor Walkway:** The Glass Floor Walkway, which provides panoramic views of the city and the River Thames, is one of the Tower Bridge's main attractions. The promenade offers a distinctive view of the city and is situated 42 meters above the river.

• **The Engine Rooms:** There are two engine rooms on the Tower Bridge, which were once used to power the bridge's raising mechanism. Visitors to the exhibit may take a tour of the engine rooms and discover more about the mechanical and technical processes at work on the bridge.

• **The Tower Bridge Dungeon:** The Tower Bridge Dungeon is a well-liked family destination that offers an entertaining and engaging way to learn about the bridge's past. Live actors, visual effects, and interactive displays are used in the dungeon to bring the history of the bridge to life.

• **Getting There:** Public transportation makes it simple to reach Tower Bridge, which is in the heart of London. The bridge is within a short distance from Tower Hill Station, which is the nearest subterranean station.

• **Hours:** Every day except Christmas Day, the Tower Bridge Exhibition is open from 9:30 am to 6 pm. It's important to get your tickets in advance since the exhibition might be crowded, particularly in the summer.

• **Dress Code:** Visitors are urged to dress correctly for the Tower Bridge Exhibition, and it's advised to avoid wearing high heels or any footwear that might harm the displays.

Overall, a trip to Tower Bridge is a must for anybody traveling to London. It offers a fascinating look into the construction and history of one of the city's most recognizable structures. There is something for everyone at the Tower Bridge, whether you are interested in the Tower Bridge Exhibition, the Glass Floor Walkway, or the Tower Bridge Dungeon.

11. Explore Camden Market: For anybody wishing to experience the alternative side of the city, this lively market is a must-visit. It is a dynamic nexus of street food, fashion, and culture.

Another of the most well-liked tourist attractions in London is Camden Market, which offers a dynamic and varied mix of food, shopping, and entertainment. The market is a well-liked hangout for both residents and tourists and is situated in the north London area of Camden. Here are some tips for visiting Camden Market:

• **Operating Hours:** The market is open every day of the week from 10:00 a.m. to 6:00 p.m., and also on weekends it is open from 9:00 a.m. to 6:00 p.m.

• **Stores and stalls:** Camden Market is home to a huge selection of shops and booths that provide everything from apparel and accessories to arts and crafts to vintage and used things. The market offers a variety of inexpensive and inexpensive products, as well as one-of-a-kind and distinctive things, to visitors.

• **Food and drink:** There are many different places to eat and drink in the market, including cafés, restaurants, and street food vendors. Along with typical British fare, visitors may sample a variety of exotic cuisines, such as Thai, Mexican, and Caribbean.

• **Entertainment:** Camden Market has a range of entertainment alternatives, including live music, street performers, and theatrical productions, in addition to eating and shopping. From reggae to ska to rock and alternative, visitors may enjoy a wide variety of entertainment.

• **Transportation:** Camden Market is conveniently close to public transportation and is situated in the north London district of Camden. The market is within a short distance from Camden Town and Chalk Farm subterranean stations, which are both nearby.

• **Safety:** It's crucial to be careful of pickpockets and keep a check on personal things while visiting Camden Market since it may be bustling and packed, particularly on weekends.

• **Parking:** Since there may not be enough parking in the Camden neighborhood, it is advised to take the bus or walk to the market. Visitors who are driving may locate paid parking in the neighborhood streets, however, it might be challenging to obtain a spot, particularly on weekends.

Anyone traveling to London should stop at Camden Market, which offers a distinctive and lively experience that is different from any other market in the city. There is something for everyone in Camden Market, whether you like food, shopping, or entertainment.

Visit the National Gallery, which has a remarkable collection of paintings from Western Europe, including pieces by Leonardo da Vinci, Sandro Botticelli, and Rembrandt.

One of the most well-liked tourist destinations in the city is the National Gallery, a famous art gallery that is situated in the center of London. Since it opened its doors in 1824, the gallery has amassed a sizable collection of Western European paintings, including works of art by masters including Leonardo da Vinci, Botticelli, Van Gogh, and Rembrandt. A guide to visiting the National Gallery is provided below:

• **Hours:** The National Gallery is open from 10:00 am to 6:00 pm, seven days a week, with later hours on Fridays. On January 1st and December 24th–26th, the museum is closed.

• **Collections:** From the 13th through the 19th centuries, the National Gallery has amassed a sizable collection of more than 2,300 paintings from Western Europe. As well as interactive exhibits and audio instructions, visitors may stroll around the galleries and examine the collection.

• **Highlights:** Among the most well-known pieces on show at the National Gallery are Rembrandt's "Self-portrait with Two Circles," Botticelli's "The Adoration of the Magi," and Leonardo da Vinci's "The Virgin of the Rocks."

• **Exhibits:** The National Gallery often presents temporary exhibitions in addition to its permanent collection. To find out what is happening when they are there, visitors may check the museum's website.

• **Guided Tours:** The National Gallery offers guided tours that provide visitors with a fantastic introduction to the collection and the background of Western European art. There are audio guides and guided tours available, and they come in a number of languages.

• **The National Café:** If you're visiting the National Gallery, here is a nice spot to get a bite to eat. The café is a terrific location to unwind and relax and provides a variety of light meals, snacks, and beverages.

• **Transportation:** The National Gallery is conveniently placed in the center of London and is accessible via public transportation. The gallery is just a short walk from Charing Cross, the nearest underground station.

Anyone with an interest in art, history, or culture should definitely pay a visit to the National Gallery. The National Gallery has something for everyone, whether you're an art enthusiast or just searching for an interesting way to spend a day in London. A trip to the National Gallery is guaranteed to be a memorable one because of its sizable collection, interactive exhibits, and breathtaking shows.

12. <u>Visit the Science Museum:</u> This museum's interactive displays and hands-on activities focus on the history of science and technology.

An internationally recognized museum devoted to the history of science and technology is located in London called the Science Museum. It is the perfect vacation spot for families and those interested in science and technology since it offers interactive displays, hands-on activities, and a sizable collection of scientific artifacts. Here are some tips for going to the Science Museum:

• **Hours:** Every day from 10 a.m. to 6 p.m., with the exception of the 24-26th of December. For any changes to the museum's operating hours, it is advised to check the website in advance.

- **Exhibitions:** The museum offers a selection of engaging interactive exhibits and hands-on activities for visitors of all ages. Visitors may study the development of communication and transportation as well as the history of science and technology, as well as uncover some of the most important scientific discoveries ever made.

- **IMAX Theater:** The Science Museum is home to one of Europe's biggest large-format IMAX theaters. A variety of educational and scientific movies, such as documentaries on nature and space, are available for viewers.

- **Temporary Exhibits:** The Science Museum also offers a variety of temporary exhibitions, each of which aims to provide a novel and engaging viewpoint on a certain topic. There is always something fresh to view since these shows are often switched up multiple times a year.

- **The Wellcome Wing:** The museum's distinct Wellcome Wing is devoted to modern science and medicine. The most recent developments in science and technology, as well as cutting-edge research and development, may be explored by visitors, who can also learn about the place of science in contemporary society.

- **The Launchpad**: A place for families and kids to connect, The Launchpad offers a variety of hands-on activities and displays that are intended to pique kids' interest and creativity.

• **Transportation:** The Science Museum is conveniently placed in the center of London and is accessible through public transportation. South Kensington, the nearest underground station, is only a short walk from the museum.

Anyone visiting London must stop by the Science Museum, which is a great place for families and those interested in science and technology. There is always something fresh and intriguing to view and explore because of the variety of interactive displays, hands-on activities, and temporary exhibitions available.

13. <u>Take a Thames River boat tour:</u> An excellent approach to explore the city from a fresh angle and obtain a distinctive picture of London's well-known sights is to take a boat trip.

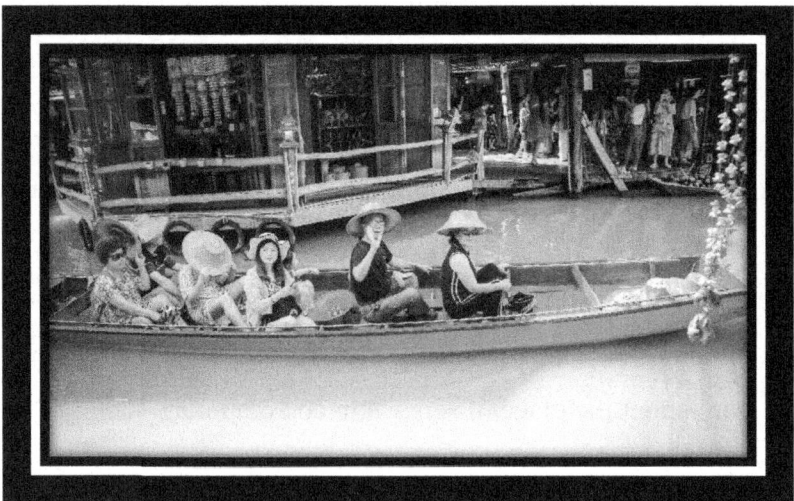

One of London's most recognizable features and a vital component of its history and culture is the River Thames. A boat excursion is a must-do for every tourist and is a fantastic opportunity to explore the city from a new angle. A guide to taking a boat excursion on the River Thames is provided below:

• **Boat Tour Types:** The River Thames offers a wide variety of boat excursions, including dinner cruises, sightseeing cruises, and themed cruises. Select the journey based on your interests and financial constraints.

• **Timing:** You may choose a boat excursion that matches your schedule since they often go on all day and into the evening. Some excursions are also offered at night, providing a unique viewpoint of the city's well-known sites.

• **Accessing the River Thames:** The River Thames runs through the center of London, and boat trip companies may be found all along the river. Embankment and Waterloo, which are both only a short walk from the river, are the nearest subterranean stations.

• **What to Visit on the Trip:** The Tower of London, the Tower Bridge, the London Eye, and the Houses of Parliament are just a few of the famous sites you'll see while taking the boat tour. Historic structures like the Tate Modern and St. Paul's Cathedral are also visible.

• **Audio Guide:** A lot of boat trips include an audio guide, which gives you important facts about the city and its sights while you float down the river.

• **Food and Drink:** Before making a reservation, be careful to confirm whether or not food and beverages are included in the boat trip.

• **Weather:** Because London's weather may be erratic, make sure to check the forecast and prepare for the weather by dressing accordingly for your boat excursion. Don't worry if it's raining; many boat cruises provide enclosed spaces where you may escape the elements.

A fantastic opportunity to view London from a new angle and discover the history and culture of the city is to take a boat trip on the River Thames. A boat trip is a must-do activity, regardless of whether you're a frequent tourist or a native.

14. <u>Visit the Victoria and Albert Museum:</u> which is focused on decorative arts and design and has a sizable collection of ceramics, textiles, and furniture in addition to current exhibits.

In South Kensington, London, there is a museum of art and design called the Victoria and Albert Museum, or the V&A. With approximately 2.3 million items ranging from pottery and textiles to furniture and fashion, the museum, founded in 1852, has one of the world's biggest and most extensive collections of decorative arts and design. A guide to visiting the Victoria & Albert Museum is provided below:

• **Hours:** The museum is free to enter and is open daily from 10:00 a.m. to 5:45 p.m. If there are any temporary closures or special exhibits that can influence hours, it is recommended to check the museum's website.

• **Collections:** The museum's broad collections span a variety of artistic and design eras and styles, from prehistoric civilizations to modern art. Visitors may visit one of the museum's many events and exhibits or browse the galleries devoted to pottery, fashion, furniture, textiles, and more.

• **Special exhibits:** The V&A often conducts special exhibitions that provide visitors the chance to see pieces of art and design that aren't typically on show. The easiest way to find out what's on and reserve tickets for these exhibits, which are often ticketed, is to visit the museum's website in advance.

• **The John Madejski Garden:** Located in the center of the museum, the John Madejski Garden is a calm sanctuary and the ideal location to unwind. Visitors may take in the stunning plants and flowers in the garden or relax on one of the numerous chairs for a picnic.

• **The V&A Café:** Located in the center of the museum, the V&A Café is a perfect location to stop for lunch or a cup of coffee. After visiting the galleries, you may relax and refuel in the café, which offers a range of light fares like croissants, sandwiches, and salads.

• **Getting There:** The South Kensington location of the Victoria and Albert Museum in London makes it simple to get there via public transportation. South Kensington and Knightsbridge are the nearest subterranean stations, both of which are close to the museum.

• **Audio Guides:** Audio guides are a terrific way to learn more about the collections and exhibits on show, and they are available for rental at the museum. The multilingual guides are a fantastic resource for tourists who wish to find out more about the museum and its holdings.

Anyone who is interested in art or design should go to the Victoria & Albert Museum.

The museum's collections and displays are likely to excite and inspire visitors, whether they are seasoned collectors or just interested. The V&A is the ideal location to spend a day exploring the world of art and design since it has something to offer everyone.

Transportation options **In the City**

CHAPTER 2: GETTING AROUND

LONDON

Transportation options in the city

Although London has an excellent public transportation system, a first-time tourist may find the abundance of options a little intimidating.

This knowledge of how to navigate London was gained from two years spent living there, additional tourist trips, and some web studies (there are so many alternatives!).

I'm going to discuss all of your alternatives for traveling to London in this chapter, including the bicycle, taxis, and the tube! Let's get going.

There are nine fare zones in London, with zones 1 and 2 being downtown London and the number of zones rising as you leave the city. For instance, The Heathrow Airport is in Zone 6. The transportation alternatives listed below will reach every zone.

TfL, or **"Transport for London,"** is the company that runs the city's transportation system. TfL is the government organization in charge of managing all facets of the London transportation network, including the roads, railways, tickets, and maintenance.

To pay for transportation inside London, you may purchase a single ticket, use a contactless card, use an Oyster card, buy a travelcard, or buy a visitor Oyster card in addition to your London Pass.

In general, if you have a contactless card that is accepted in the UK, this is now the best option, followed by the Oyster card. I have produced a whole guide on how to pay for transportation in London, which you can read by clicking on the next heading.

1. Underground – "The Tube"

With portions operational since 1863, the London Underground, or "Tube," is the world's oldest underground metro network. With 270 stations and 250 miles of track, the London Underground now handles over a billion people annually. Interestingly, despite the name, less than 50% of the music is truly subterranean.

You will often find an underground station within easy walking distance and a train coming in 10 minutes or less in the bulk of London. The underground is one of the most effective methods to travel about and is often the greatest option since it doesn't have to worry about traffic and streets.

The majority of services run from 5 a.m. to midnight, however starting in August 2016 several lines will also provide a 24-hour service.

The recognizable London Underground emblem, a red circle with the word "Underground" inside in a blue box, makes tube stations simple to identify.

The London Underground is divided into fare zones 1 through 6, with zone 1 being in the center and zone 6 on the outside. In general, your trip will cost more the more zones you pass through.

The majority of tube stations have barriers at the entrance and exit, and you may buy tickets at the station via machines or ticket booths.

As a piece of advice, avoid using the Underground during rush hour on weekdays if you're a tourist to London since it becomes quite packed with commuters. From Monday through Friday, this often occurs between 7:30 and 8:30 in the morning and 4:30 to 7:00 in the evening.

Additionally, with direct connections from each of the Heathrow terminals to downtown London, the tube is the most economical method to get between Heathrow Airport and the city.

2. Overground

Similar to the Underground, but above the earth, is the Overground. I am aware that the Underground has a number of above-ground areas. That is the way things are. Though much more recent than the Underground, the Overground was founded in 2007 and fills in some of the Underground's coverage gaps.

The Overground charges the same fares as the Underground and operates under the same zone-based regulations.

In most situations, you do not need to tap in and out when going from Overground to Underground services if you are using Oyster or contactless payment since they are in the same tariff zone, however, there are certain stations where this is necessary.

The only difference between the Overground and Underground logos is that the Overground's circle is orange and its title is different.

3. DLR (Docklands Light Railway)

I love London. And we're just on the third choice in terms of transportation! The docklands district of London, which is the region immediately east and southeast of central London, is covered by the automated rail system known as the Docklands Light

Railway, or DLR as it is more often known. The key distinction between this train system and others mentioned before is that there are no drivers since the DLR is totally automated.

You'll probably use the DLR if you're traveling through east and south-east London since it connects London City Airport to the rest of the subway system. For instance, it is the finest method of transportation to the ExCeL, which is home to several sizable events and trade exhibitions.

The DLR has the same rates as the Overground and Underground and is included in the same general London price zone. In fact, several tube stations also include DLR stops.

You don't have to touch in and out when changing from the tube to the DLR if you're using an Oyster or contactless payment, but you should be aware that many DLR stations lack barriers, so you must remember to touch in and out (or have a valid ticket) at the beginning and end of your journey to ensure you pay the correct fare.

4. Rail Services

Yes, I've previously covered three rail-like services, but in case you missed it, London also has genuine railroads, including suburban rail that connects the city's center to its suburbs and fast trains that connect it to the rest of the nation (and the world).

Generally speaking, trains into and out of London are not part of the Transport for London system. As a result, you cannot use your Oyster card on the bulk of national rail services and must pay for a different ticket.

There are several exceptions, such as the fact that zones 1 through 9 and a few specific destinations are covered for all suburban trains. The Oyster system also has coverage for trains to Gatwick, such as the Gatwick Express, as well as Heathrow, such as the Elizabeth Line and Heathrow Express.

5. Bus

The Underground is perhaps the most popular mode of public transportation in London if you ask someone. And that's not a terrible estimate given the more than a billion consumers every year. However, that would be incorrect given that there are more than two billion bus trips in London every year.

This is probably because there are so many bus lines in London that cover such a large area, making it possible to get almost everywhere in the city by bus. Bus fares are also less expensive for Oyster users, with a set charge of £1.65 (as of February 2023) for a single trip, no matter the distance.

With Oyster and contactless cards, you can additionally benefit from the "hopper" rate, which includes the cost of every bus trip you take within an hour after tapping in. Therefore, you may change buses without paying any additional fees. However, in order for your ticket to be valid, you still need to touch the new bus.

You just need to tap your Oyster or contactless card on the giant yellow card reader when you board the bus in London to utilize the public transportation system; there is no need to do so when you exit since tariffs are set. Additionally, a lot of bus lines run around the clock, so you may often use public transportation to get home after a night out.

Because of the traffic, they must deal with, which is often very bad in London, buses are typically a bit slower than train services. The fact that there are often no stairs and short treks throughout the Underground system is a benefit.

It is possible to ride a Hop on Hop off a bus in addition to a public bus. Even though they aren't considered public transportation, they may be a convenient means of transportation for tourists visiting London since they stop at the city's top tourist sights and provide commentary. They are, however, charged individually and are, unsurprisingly, more costly than a regular bus.

6. Tram

The London Tramlink tram route runs throughout south London, especially from Wimbledon to Croydon and Beckenham. Despite having just four lines and 17 miles of track, the tram is a popular transportation option in the area.

Payment for the tram is the same as for the bus; there is a set fare for each trip, and you just touch in with your Oyster card or contactless card to confirm your ticket as you board. When you get off the ship, you don't have to touch out. The Hopper ticket structure also includes fares for trams.

7. Emirates Air Line

Let's move on to something a little more unique. Did you know there is a cable car service in London? The only urban cable car in the UK, it transports passengers from Greenwich to the Royal Victoria Dock over the River Thames.

It provides panoramic views of this area of the city as you cross and is a convenient route to travel to the ExCeL exhibition center and the O2 Arena from the south side of the river.

You may use your Oyster card or contactless card to make a purchase at The Air Line as it uses the TfL system. It's also one of the simplest types of public transportation in London to use since there are just two stations—one at each end.

8. River Boat

Given that London is traversed by a large, ancient river, it seems reasonable that this canal serves as a means of public transportation. As a result, Thames Clippers is carrying out service with permission from TfL.

There are four "routes," with the first one beginning in Putney in the extreme west and ending in Woolwich in the far east. In essence, you can go from one end of London to the other using this.

It's a pleasant, picturesque route that is often a bit less congested than many of the other options. However, as commuters utilize it, peak hours may be a bit busier. The simplest method of payment, as with other TfL services, is with an Oyster or Contactless card that you touch in and out as you board and disembark.

Alternatively, you may purchase tickets at the pier in person or online and print them off. The final option is the most costly; the most affordable ticketing options are contactless, Oyster, and online.

Noting that the Thames Clipper is somewhat more costly than services like the subway or buses, it may be worth it given the point-to-point service, reasonable speed, and views of London from the river.

If you decide to purchase the money-saving attraction pass for your stay in London, the London Pass also comes with a 24-hour pass.

9. Taxis

London has many recognizable transportation options, including the tube and the fabled red bus. But the black cab is arguably the most well-known of all.

London's Hackney Carriages, which have a history dating back to 1662, have been transporting people around the city for more than 350 years. Drivers are required to learn the infamous "Knowledge," which is essentially a detailed map of London so they can navigate the city effectively without using maps or technology.

The experience of riding in a black cab in London is unquestionable. The driver will stop to pick you up if you wave at one and signal that one is available (if it is, the taxi light will be illuminated).

Although black taxis are undoubtedly more expensive than any of the other modes of transportation governed by TfL, they can oftentimes be the most convenient option for getting around the city, especially if you're traveling with others.

Taxi fares must be paid with cash or a credit card because Oyster cards are not accepted in taxis. The fare is paid at the end of the trip and is calculated using the meter in the cab based on the distance and time.

10. Bicycles

The bicycle was introduced as a new mode of transportation in London in 2010! There are public bike racks located all over the city, and with the expansion of cycle lanes, these are becoming a well-liked mode of transportation for quick trips.

It's not difficult to rent a bike; the fee of £1.65 includes 24 hours of system access and 30 minutes of actual riding time. Each additional segment of 30 minutes after the first 30 costs £1.65.

If you anticipate using the cycles frequently, a £20 membership will grant you access for one month with unlimited rides of up to 60 minutes each; any additional 60 minutes will cost you £1.65.

All you need to use the cycle rental system is a credit or debit card. The system does not accept Oyster cards due to the need to prevent theft. You can access bicycles at locations all over the city after paying your activation fee with a card. There are literally hundreds of them to choose from.

Please take note that the above prices only apply to standard bicycles. E-bikes are also offered but at a higher cost and only to registered users.

11. Walking

Though it's not exactly a form of public transportation, walking is still a viable option for getting around London. Many tourists are unaware of how pedestrian-friendly many areas of London are; in fact, in central London, you can walk to the majority of the attractions.

It's usually quicker to walk if it's less than two tube stops away, though it's always a good idea to check the map to make sure there isn't a river in the way! The cheapest and most convenient way for us to get around London is on foot.

Accessibility on Public Transport in London

The accessibility situation is undoubtedly diverse in London given the variety of available public transportation alternatives. Buses are an excellent example; every route is served by low-floor vehicles and has a spot for wheelchairs.

On the other side, the tube isn't the best for step-free access, with just around a fifth of stations providing it. Even while improvements are being made, an outdated network that was constructed before accessibility was a factor has not helped. There are certain stations with a platform for street step-free access, however, your tube trip has to be properly planned.

Which mode of transportation around London is best?

There isn't really a simple method to respond to this query. The Underground will probably be the most practical method of transportation if you want to go around most of downtown London. It moves quickly, often, and is unaffected by traffic.

The tube map isn't geographically accurate, so it's worth looking up the real walking distance before using the tube. So, there are situations when walking is really faster.

The bus is the next most practical choice for areas of London that aren't covered by the Underground, DLR, or Overground services. The city has full of services, many of which are available 24/7.

Cycling or walking are both excellent options if you don't mind getting a little exercise while getting about.

The Thames Clippers or the Emirates Air Line will provide something different if you wish to try it.

The latter may be a terrific method to move throughout London with sea views, while the former is unquestionably wonderful for a single route. However, in my opinion, the latter is more of an experience than something that a tourist would use often.

How To Pay In London For Public Transportation

The most effective means of transportation in London is covered right at the start of this chapter. That is all well and good, but it is lacking a crucial element: the most economical method of paying for transportation in London.

You may assume that the answer to this question would be rather simple, but it's really a little more difficult than you might expect. Do not worry, though; this feature will walk you through your choices and assist you in selecting the best payment method for utilizing London's public transportation system.

First, the bulk of London's public transportation may be paid for in three different ways. These are cash, a contactless-enabled credit or debit card, and the London Oyster Card. Let's briefly review each of these three possibilities before deciding which is best for you.

Travelers in London Have Three Payment Options: Cash, Contactless, and Oyster

Cash – With the exception of taxis, cash is by far the worst method of payment for transportation in London and should be avoided at all costs (although these accept contactless and credit cards too).

Cash fares are often far more expensive than the other methods of payment, and certain services, like the bus, no longer even take cash. Basically, if you can help it, avoid paying for your ticket in cash in London.

The best choice is to get an Oyster Card if you must spend cash. At the majority of stations, they may be bought and topped up with cash. Just be sure you go to a ticket desk or a machine that takes cash.

Oyster Card – The Oyster card is a reloadable, widely used card that may be used on all modes of transportation around London. There are other variations of this card, but for the sake of this Chapter, we'll concentrate on the common blue Oyster card, which is available in London at the majority of rail and tube stations.

Contactless – A bank-issued credit or debit card that has been activated for contactless transactions is now the most recent method of payment for transportation in London. This indicates that the card has a chip that can be wirelessly read when it is held up to a contactless reader.

You may use these cards for everyday purchases as well as to pay for transportation in London using contactless cards. These may be used in place of cash payments or Oyster cards for purchasing tickets. You may also use this as a contactless payment option if your smartphone supports Apple Pay or Google Pay.

These are the three possibilities. In order to determine which method is ideal for you while paying for travel in London, we'll concentrate on the Oyster Card and Contactless Cards in this piece.

We're going to disregard cash as a payment option in this article and urge you to do the same since it is expensive to purchase tickets with cash and just a few transportation alternatives even take it.

Oyster Cards vs. Contactless for Travel in London

Which London public transportation systems enable contactless payments?

Currently, contactless payment methods may be used to board the bus, tube, tram, DLR, London Overground, Emirates Air Line, River Bus, and the bulk of London-bound National Rail services.

Some airport services, such as Gatwick Express and Heathrow Express, also accept contactless payments.

If the fare is less than the contactless threshold of £100, you may also use contactless to pay for any black cabs. Black cabs should be noted as being distinct from other types of public transportation in London and being charged accordingly; they are not included in travel cards, caps, or other payment plans.

In general, you can use a contactless card anyplace you can now use an Oyster card - simply search for the yellow Oyster card reader and remember to touch in (and out, if required) to pay for your trip.

Advantages of Contactless

You already have a contactless credit card or smartphone that supports it, so using it for your trip is more convenient than buying a separate Oyster card, which requires a deposit and maintenance fees.

Does not need charging: Oyster's preload method, which requires credit to be loaded onto the card before usage, is one of its key drawbacks. It can be configured to refresh itself automatically, but if you're a visitor to London, the added bother may not be worthwhile.

Instead, you'll find yourself waiting in line at refill stations at tube stops, and if you run out of credit at a bus stop—which is likely—you won't have much luck since few bus stops have recharge points.

Since contactless cards are connected to your bank account, you'll always be good to go as long as you have credit.

You may make payments with a mobile app using Google Pay or Apple Pay: You can connect your contactless card to your smartphone payment system and use it instead of carrying a contactless card if your smartphone enables contactless payments.

Can be less expensive in certain circumstances: Due to a change in how daily capping works between zones, Contactless can sometimes be a little less expensive for daily tickets, particularly if you are traveling from a more remote part of London. This doesn't generally make a large impact, but it sometimes can make contactless a little bit less expensive for everyday commutes.

Disadvantages of Contactless

Not all foreign-issued cards are supported: Using UK-issued contactless-enabled Visa, Mastercard, Maestro, and American Express cards to pay for your London transportation should be no trouble.

Unfortunately, requirements seem to be different for contactless cards issued abroad. All American Express contactless cards should function properly right now. Then, certain Mastercard, Maestro, and

Visa cards issued abroad will function, while others won't. There isn't a definite list; you just have to give it a go.

Foreign transaction fees: Even if the Oyster contactless system supports a card issued abroad, you should check to see whether there are any foreign transaction fees before using the card.

Because contactless transactions are made in GBP, if your card issuer charges you transaction fees for purchases made in another currency, these expenses may negate the savings from contactless. Before you leave, confirm with your card's issuer to check whether this is the case.

Concessions can't be added: The lack of support for concessions, such as those for elders, students, and young children, is a significant drawback of contactless.

You should utilize Oyster cards or travelcards to enjoy cheap travel, including with the Young Visitors Discount, which provides 50% off travel when loaded to an Oyster card, if you're a tourist to London traveling with kids between the ages of 11 and 15.

If an adult pays the fee, a child under the age of 11 travels for free. Contactless is compatible with this policy. You will just need to utilize the bigger ticket barriers (designated for baggage or those with disabilities) at tube stations so you may pass through together.

Which public transportation in London accepts Oyster?

Oyster is compatible with all of London's public transportation alternatives, including the bus, tube, tram, DLR, London Overground, Emirates Air Line, River Bus, and the vast majority of National Rail services operating inside the city.

Keep in mind that in London, a black cab cannot be paid for using an Oyster card.

The Hop on Hop off bus service, which you would have to pay extra for, does not accept the Oyster Card either.

If you want to do a lot of sightseeing while in the city, a card like the London Pass that includes Hop on Hop Off transportation alternatives can be a suitable choice.

Advantages of Oyster

It functions, and assistance is offered. While it has been reported that not all contactless cards are compatible with the system, the Oyster card should always function. If there are issues, if your card is registered on the TfL website, you may seek help or have your credit reimbursed.

Spending is simpler to keep track of since you have to load your Oyster card, which makes it simpler to monitor your spending and establish spending limits.

Although the ordinary person won't notice much of a difference from this since they will probably need to travel anyway, it is something to keep in mind if you prefer to limit your spending on public transportation.

Supports travelcards: The Oyster card's compatibility with travelcards is one of its key benefits. These are fixed-price, pre-paid solutions that allow for unrestricted travel within predetermined London zones for a weekly, monthly, or yearly fee.

This benefit has diminished due to weekly fare capping since the cost of a seven-day travelcard on Oyster is equal to the weekly maximum on contactless. While contactless capping is set for Monday through Sunday, a seven-day Oyster transit card is valid for seven days after activation, regardless of the day of the week.

It will be more cost-effective than a contactless card if you are in London for seven days beginning at any time other than the Monday through Sunday period and will be traveling enough to make the travel card worthwhile.

Supports cash: You may purchase and top up an Oyster card with cash if you wish to pay for your transportation in London with cash.

With the unusual exception of a one-off, single trip, this is often far more affordable than purchasing a cash ticket since you don't have to pay for the Oyster card.

Supports concessions: As was said above, in order to obtain the greatest bargain on transportation in London, if you are traveling with children or are a resident of London who is eligible for one of the discounts or concessions offered to adults, you should use the Oyster card that corresponds to your concession. You may also add a Young Tourist discount to an Oyster card for discounts if you're a visitor to London with kids between the ages of 11 and 15.

Visitor Oyster Card Discounts: You are eligible for various savings if you purchase a visiting Oyster card before your trip to the UK, such as the one that comes with the London Pass. The whole list is available here. Although I wouldn't suggest that they are reasons to purchase the card particularly, it is still useful to be aware of them.

Disadvantages of Oyster

You have to pay a deposit: A £5 deposit is required when you initially acquire an Oyster card. Since 2020, this £5 has been transferred to the card as credit a year after your purchase, when it used to be refundable. This may not be a credit you can use if you are only in London for a short period, thus utilizing it will really cost you £5.

It has to be recharged: Oyster's primary drawback is that it's a pay-as-you-go card that requires credit to use. This is OK if you commute mostly by tube since most tube stations have machines you can top up at. However, if you often use the bus—often the most economical way to get to London—you'll have to look hard for a charging station since the majority of bus stops don't have one. By setting up auto top-up when you register your card online, you may avoid this problem.

Can't be used on taxis: Although it's not a major problem, it's worth remembering that your Oyster card cannot be used for cabs. We'd really advise against using a cab unless you truly need to go directly from point A to point B due to the increased costs involved, but we've included it just the same.

There will always be money left over: Oyster is a pay-as-you-go system, therefore in order to use it, the card must have money on it. It's very hard to bring the card to zero since travel fees differ. There will be money left on the card if you stop using it. By returning the card, you can receive this money back, but we have a feeling that most people won't. According to TfL, there are approximately £400 million in unclaimed balances and deposits as of 2019!

Should You Pay for London Public Transportation with Contactless or Oyster?

First off, don't worry too much about attempting to obtain a contactless payment card just for the trip to London if you're visiting London and don't already have one; the Oyster system will work just fine for you.

In most circumstances, you should use your contactless-enabled credit or debit card to pay for transportation in London if it is accepted by the city's transportation system. It's the simplest and most practical method of payment, accepted on all modes of transportation, and often costs less or the same as using an Oyster card.

You should generally avoid using your contactless card when:

1. In the event that your card was not issued in the UK and your card issuer charged you fees for international transactions, making it more expensive than Oyster

2. If you qualify for a concession, such as if you're a senior person living in London or you're traveling with kids between the ages of 11 and 15.

3. If you purchase a weekly 7-day travelcard to only trip outside of Zone 1 (unlikely as a visitor to London)

4. If you are purchasing a weekly 7-day travelcard and your vacation is for a week-long period that is not from Monday

to Sunday, you will travel enough to reach the daily limit on at least five out of those seven days.

5. There is no monthly capping if you purchase a monthly travelcard for use in London and contactless makes this impossible.

There are undoubtedly more instances when a travelcard or Oyster card will be less expensive than a contactless one. Normally, to figure this out, you'll need to perform some arithmetic and have a thorough grasp of your precise travel arrangements, which may take more time than is necessary to save a little money.

Outside of the five criteria mentioned above, we think that if you're a tourist, you'll find that using a contactless for your journey in London is generally both more convenient and less expensive if you already have a contactless card. If any of those situations apply to you, you may either purchase an Oyster card in advance of your visit or after you arrive.

Therefore, if any of the aforementioned five situations don't apply to you, we advise using your contactless card to travel in London. It's simple and handy, you don't have to bother about charging it, and you get to take advantage of daily and weekly travel limits, so it's almost always going to be less expensive than the other choices for most visitors to London.

Is Weekly Capping Supported by Oyster?

Only contactless supported weekly fare capping on the whole network to the end of September 2021. In order to ensure that you never spend more for travel than you would have if you had bought a one-day travel card, both Oyster and Contactless have long supported daily capping. However, up until September 2021, only Contactless supported the Monday through Sunday weekly limit.

The TfL network will begin supporting daily and weekly limits starting on September 28, 2021, which is fantastic news for Oyster card holders as it may result in considerable savings.

For instance, the current weekly maximum is £37 if all of your travel takes place in zones 1 and 2. It is better if your trip begins on a Monday since this weekly limit is computed for travel from Monday through Sunday. Zones 1 and 2 have a daily limit of £7.40, for comparison. That is £51.80 when spread out over a week.

Advice on how to use your payment method

Make sure you stay with your chosen payment method after choosing it, whether it be a contactless, Oyster, or smartphone payment system. Only swipe that payment method on the scanner. If you hold two payment options close to the terminal, it will randomly choose one of them, which means that if you don't tap out with the same card, you can be charged twice.

Make sure you constantly use your smartphone to pay if you are using a Google or Apple device. It is theoretically recorded as a separate payment card if you have a payment card registered on the device and choose to use the real card rather than the smartphone, or vice versa.

If you and a friend are traveling together and you only have one contactless payment card, this is really a decent solution. One person may use the physical card while the other uses the smartphone version by adding the card to an Apple or Google device.

Additionally, we strongly advise you to register your payment method online with TfL. This has several advantages, such as allowing you to keep track of your spending and, in the case of an Oyster card, allowing you to recover any monies on it in event of loss!

Neighborhoods to consider for your accommodation

CHAPTER 3: WHERE TO STAY IN

LONDON

Neighborhoods to consider for your accommodation

It's crucial to think about the area you want to be in when deciding where to stay in London. Here are five well-liked areas to think about for your accommodation:

Mayfair: One of London's most affluent districts, Mayfair is home to some of the city's best inns, eateries, and stores. It's a fantastic choice for anyone who wishes to be near the city's center while yet living in luxury.

One of the most prestigious neighborhoods in the city is Mayfair, which is situated in London's West End. It is a well-liked option for visitors seeking a high-end experience in London because of its upmarket environment and opulent facilities.

Mayfair's shopping, which includes some of London's best boutiques and designer stores, is one of its primary draws. With its upscale jewelry stores, fashionable boutiques, and art galleries, Bond Street is a particularly well-liked retail area.

Some of London's best restaurants, serving anything from traditional British meals to foreign cuisine, can be found in Mayfair. There are many alternatives in Mayfair, whether you're searching for a Michelin-starred eating establishment or a more relaxed supper.

Mayfair has a variety of lodging alternatives, including anything from five-star hotels to serviced residences. Mayfair is home to The Ritz London, The Dorchester, and Claridge's, three of the city's most opulent hotels.

With many London Underground stations situated inside the area, including Green Park, Bond Street, and Oxford Circus, Mayfair is also well-linked to the rest of the city. This makes it simple to go to and see other parts of the city while still taking advantage of Mayfair's opulence and exclusivity.

Mayfair, with its opulent facilities, sophisticated ambiance, and convenient location, is a fantastic choice for visitors seeking a high-end experience in London. If you're in town for business or pleasure, this upscale neighborhood has a lot to offer.

Kensington: Kensington is a wealthy area that attracts both locals and visitors. The Victoria and Albert Museum, the Natural History Museum, and some of London's top retail avenues, notably High Street Kensington, arc all located there.

The Royal Borough of Kensington and Chelsea contains the area of Kensington, which is renowned for its rich environment and well-off citizens. Due to the abundance of activities, shopping possibilities, and convenient transportation, it is a well-liked vacation spot for both individuals and families.

The museums in Kensington, including some of London's most well-known museums, are among the neighborhood's principal attractions. Anyone interested in art, design, or culture must visit the Victoria & Albert Museum, one of the biggest and most comprehensive design museums in the world. Another well-liked destination is the Natural History Museum, which has a significant collection of specimens and specimens, including dinosaurs, animals, and insects.

Kensington's lively commercial areas, such as High Street Kensington, which provide a variety of shopping opportunities, are another feature. There are many options in Kensington, whether you're seeking high-end designer boutiques, distinctive independent stores, or high-street brands.

With many London Underground stations situated inside the area, notably High Street Kensington, South Kensington, and Earl's Court, Kensington is very well linked to the rest of the city. This makes it simple to get to and explore other parts of the city while still being able to enjoy Kensington's residential vibe.

With its wealthy ambiance, cultural attractions, and fantastic shopping opportunities, Kensington is a fantastic choice for visitors seeking a well-rounded experience in London. The Kensington neighborhood is definitely worth taking into consideration whether you're traveling with your family or are just searching for a handy location to stay in the city.

Soho: Soho is a vibrant area with a variety of pubs, clubs, and theaters that is well-known for its nightlife. It is a terrific choice for people who wish to be in the center of the city's cultural scene and is also home to some of London's greatest eateries. For people who prefer being in the thick of things, Soho is the perfect area since it is lively and energetic.

The West End of London has the Soho area, which is renowned for its lively and cosmopolitan vibe. With a variety of pubs, clubs, and theaters to pick from, it is one of the most well-liked nightlife districts in the city. You may choose from a variety of activities in Soho, including seeing a performance, dancing the night away, and having a drink with friends.

Soho is home to some of London's greatest restaurants, providing a variety of culinary types from traditional British food to foreign delicacies, in addition to its vibrant nightlife. With its abundance of upscale eateries and more affordable eating alternatives, Soho is a fantastic location to discover the city's culinary culture.

In addition to having a number of museums and art galleries inside its borders, Soho is renowned for its live music venues and theaters. It's a fantastic choice for individuals who wish to experience a vibrant ambiance while being in the center of the city's cultural scene.

Soho has a variety of lodging choices, ranging from high-end hotels to hostels that are affordable. The Soho Hotel, Radisson Blu Edwardian Mercer Street, and The Soho House are some of the most well-known lodging options in Soho.

With many London Underground stations situated inside the area, including Oxford Circus, Tottenham Court Road, and Piccadilly Circus, Soho is well-linked to the rest of the city. This makes it simple to get to and see other parts of the city while still taking advantage of Soho's buzz and bustle.

With its exciting nightlife, fantastic food choices, and cultural activities, Soho is a fantastic choice for visitors seeking a dynamic and cultural experience in London. This thriving area has a lot to offer, whether you're visiting for a night out or a cultural excursion.

The fashionable district of Camden: Is well-known for its alternative and bohemian lifestyle. Along with a variety of small stores and eateries, it is home to various street markets, including Camden Market and Buck Street Market. It's a fantastic choice for people seeking a distinctive and odd experience in London.

The North London area of Camden is well-known for its alternative and bohemian lifestyle. With a variety of street markets, small stores, and distinctive eating choices that cater to a wide range of tastes, it offers a lively and varied vibe.

Camden Market, a street market that has long been a fixture of the area, is one of the most well-known sights in Camden. There are several vendors there that offer anything from handcrafted goods to jewelry and antique clothes and accessories. It's a fantastic area to get a snack while exploring since there are many food vendors there serving a variety of cuisines.

Other street markets in Camden include Buck Street Market and Stables Market, where you can find a variety of small stores and booths offering one-of-a-kind goods. You may discover something of interest in Camden whether you're seeking for handcrafted crafts, antique apparel, or one-of-a-kind gifts.

The area is also home to a wide choice of eateries, cafés, and pubs that serve food from across the world as well as classic British fare. There are many alternatives in Camden, whether you're looking for a quick lunch, a big breakfast, or a sophisticated evening.

Camden has a variety of lodging alternatives, from more expensive hotels to hostels that are more affordable. Several serviced apartments are also available in the area, giving those who like it more room and solitude.

For those seeking an unusual and eccentric experience in London, Camden is a terrific choice. It's a neighborhood that has something to offer everyone with its alternative culture, street markets, local stores, and dynamic food scene.

Greenwich: The historic district of Greenwich is situated outside of London. There are several parks and open areas there as well as the Royal Observatory and the Cutty Sark. It's a fantastic choice for people seeking a more laid-back ambiance while yet being conveniently close to the city core.

Southeast London's Greenwich district is renowned for its maritime heritage and long history. The Royal Observatory, the birthplace of the Prime Meridian and the origin of Greenwich Mean Time, is one of its many well-known attractions.

One of Greenwich's primary draws is its parks and green areas, which include the Royal Park, which gives breathtaking views of the city skyline, and the famed Greenwich Market, a favorite spot for eating and shopping.

The Cutty Sark, a 19th-century clipper ship that has been refurbished and is now accessible to tourists as a museum, is also located in Greenwich. Explore the complex features and the inside of the ship at this one-of-a-kind attraction to learn more about maritime history.

The DLR (Docklands Light Railway) and the riverboat service, which provide quick and easy access to the city center, are two transportation choices that link the area to the rest of the city.

From affordable hostels and bed & breakfasts to opulent hotels and serviced apartments, Greenwich offers a variety of lodging options. It's a fantastic choice for those who want to see a more genuine and local side of London while yet being close to the city's biggest attractions.

Greenwich is a neighborhood that has something to offer everyone, regardless of your interests in history, nature, or just wanting to get away from the rush of the city. So, if you want to have a special and unforgettable experience while visiting London, think about finding lodging in this quaint and ancient area.

Types of accommodation available in the city

Visitors visiting London may choose from a broad variety of lodging alternatives since the city is huge and varied. The following are some of the most prevalent kinds of lodging available in the city:

HOTELS

There are many hotels in London to choose from, from luxurious facilities to more affordable ones. Hotels may be found practically everywhere in the city, and they are available in various sizes and forms, from modest bed and breakfasts to substantial global chains.

A chic boutique-style room in the center of the city can be yours at these reasonably priced luxury hotels in London for not much more than £100 a night. Each of these hotel companies, which are often tiny chains with a few sites across the city, has focused on providing affordable rooms while eliminating extraneous amenities like gyms or business centers.

But if you want an inexpensive hotel in London that has premium bedding, modern furnishings, and artwork, as well as a few opulent amenities, you don't have to forgo elegance. This makes them my first picks for accommodations in London.

THE RESIDENT

The Resident, formerly known as the Nadler, has four locations in London: Soho, Kensington, Covent Garden, and Victoria. By cutting all the hotel amenities, they can provide four-star accommodations at a reasonable price. The rooms, which also include extra luxuries like Nespresso machines, Brita water filters, and local discount cards, are now the main emphasis.

There is a selection of room types, including single, tiny double, regular double, king, superior, deluxe, and suites. The room types vary significantly depending on the location. Since all of them have free WiFi, free UK phone calls, air conditioning, original artwork, and Gilchrist & Soames amenities, the only real variation between them is the size of the rooms.

One feature I cherished was the little kitchen that had a microwave, sink, kettle, and refrigerator, plus silverware and crockery in each room. Therefore, making your own breakfast or ordering takeout is simple. You may also order food or beverages to be brought to your room.

The Victoria Resident is across from Buckingham Palace and a 10-minute walk from Victoria Coach and Tube Stations.

The pubs and eateries of Soho encircle The Resident Soho, which is located immediately south of Oxford Street. Additionally, the Royal Opera House and West End theaters are accessible from the Resident Covent Garden. All hotels include a 24-hour front desk where their "Resident Insiders" may direct visitors to places to dine and drink, make transport and tour arrangements, and more.

Z HOTELS

Z Hotels are yet another smart, convenient choice. They offer 11 sites in London and advertise themselves as "The Urbanite Stay." Although small, rooms are cleverly planned to maximize space and concentrate on the necessities, such as high-quality bedding and strong showers.

If you want to be close to the action and won't be in your room for long, these cheap hotels in London are ideal. Along with wheelchair-accessible accommodations, there are single, small double, and bigger queen rooms available. The inside double rooms without a window are the cheapest and start at between £60 and £70, depending on where you are.

Each room has a 40-inch HD TV, free WiFi, and a wet room with a glass wall and Thierry Mugler amenities. Each hotel also has an associated Z Café and bar that sells sandwiches, snacks, and beverages after serving a buffet breakfast each morning.

The Z Hotel Victoria is situated across from Victoria railway and tube station. Near the Holborn Underground Station, on Kingsway, lies the Z Hotel Holborn. South of Oxford Street, among Soho clubs and West End theaters, are the Soho and Tottenham Court Road branches.

The Covent Garden, Strand, and Trafalgar branches are adjacent to the Strand, Covent Garden market, and Charing Cross and can be reached on foot in a few minutes. Additionally, Leicester Square and the National Gallery are accessible from the Z Hotel Piccadilly.

Near Temple station and the Inns of Court, on Fleet Street, lies the City hotel. There are several hip pubs all around the Z Hotel Shoreditch, which is close to Old Street station. Additionally, the Gloucester Place hotel is near Hyde Park and Marylebone station.

CITIZENM

Three CitizenM hotels may be found in the heart of London. They are renowned for their eccentric design, which features vibrant colors, contemporary artwork, and chic furniture. Hotels often offer a community lounge where guests may relax away from their rooms, where they can borrow books and laptops and purchase food and beverages at the on-site restaurant.

There is just one kind of accommodation available, which has a king-sized bed, an en suite bathroom with a rain shower, and wall-to-wall windows to maximize the view (or blackout blinds to keep it out). The ambient lighting in the rooms and the app that controls the TV, temperature, blinds, and lighting give them a high-tech atmosphere. Free internet and on-demand movies are also available.

The CitizenM Bankside is situated directly south of the Thames, adjacent to Borough Market, Southwark railway, and the Tate Modern art museum. A short distance from Tower Hill Underground station and just behind the tower lies the Tower of London hotel. The Shard and the Thames may be seen from some of the rooms, and there is a rooftop pub with a balcony and expansive views.

The CitizenM Shoreditch is a short distance from Old Spitalfields Market and Boxpark Shoreditch. Liverpool Street and Shoreditch overground stations are also nearby. In addition, a fourth CitizenM hotel is scheduled to debut in 2022 close to Victoria Station.

THE CORNER

The Corner hotel in East London, which was formerly managed by the Dutch company Qbic, prides itself on being the city's greenest lodging option. They employ organic beds and toiletries, LED lighting, solar panels, low-flow shower heads, and sustainably sourced and repurposed furniture, and low-flow shower heads to reduce their water and electricity use.

To maximize space, rooms are designed like pods and include king-sized beds, workstations with storage, mood lighting, and high-speed internet in addition to colorful artwork.

THE CORNER LONDON CITY HOTEL

There are three main accommodation types: plush rooms, normal doubles, and snug rooms (doubles without windows) (large doubles with a sofa bed which can sleep three adults or two adults and two kids). There are additional rooms that are accessible.

The hotel includes a Bar + Kitchen that serves food and beverages made from sustainable sources. On each level, there is also complimentary tea and coffee. Between Whitechapel and Algate in the East End, the Qbic London City is conveniently close to Shoreditch and the Tower of London.

IBIS STYLES

IBIS STYLES With locations all over the globe, including four in the heart of London, ibis Styles is the hipper, younger sibling of the ibis hotel brand. Each of the hotels has a distinctive style with a unique idea that draws influence from its surroundings.

Queen-size or twin beds are available in the rooms at these chic, inexpensive hotels in London. Additionally, some single rooms and bigger, premium accommodations with extras like Nespresso machines and couch beds are available. Additionally, they cater to families with four-person family rooms, play spaces in the lobby, and extras like bottle warmers and high chairs.

There are bars in each hotel, and the Southwark and Excel locations also offer restaurants. In close proximity to London Bridge and Borough Market lies the ibis Styles Southwark. Also in East London, next to the Excel exposition center, O2 concert hall, and London City Airport, is the Excel hotel.

The Natural History Museum is a five-minute walk from the Gloucester Road Hotel in Kensington, which is located across from the Gloucester Road Underground Station. And only a few minutes to the west, next to Earl's Court station, is the ibis Styles Kensington.

POINT A

Try Point A Hotels, which has seven hotels around London and offers rooms beginning at £59 per night, if you don't need fancy features and simply want a cheap yet stylish place for the night.

Simple options include double or twin rooms with or without windows, accessible versions with adapted toilets, and space for a wheelchair.

Comfortable Hypnos beds, under-bed storage, a drop-down desk, a smart TV, mood lighting, air conditioning, and power showers help rooms make the most of their available space. They have incredibly handy locations and offer an excellent spot to sleep if you are out and about touring London, according to my experience staying in a few of their hotels.

If you have an early train, Eurostar, or flight to catch, their King's Cross St. Pancras, Paddington, and Liverpool Street hotels are ideal because they are next to the corresponding stations.

The Houses of Parliament are located across the river from Point A Westminster. Earl's Court and Olympia are near the Kensington location. Old Street station is not far from The Point A Shoreditch. Additionally, Docklands and the Museum of London are accessible from the Canary Wharf hotel.

<u>Suggestions For Finding Cheap Hotels In London</u>

Reserve in advance: Since there aren't many cheap hotels in London and it's constantly crowded, making reservations in advance will save you money. Research has shown that the sweet spot for the lowest pricing is around 30 days before your vacation, which is not too long in advance.

Subscribe to mailing lists: Join their mailing list if there is a certain hotel or chain you wish to visit to learn about deals and discounts. Some businesses provide memberships where customers may save money by signing up, such as The Resident, which offers members a 15% discount on accommodations. Additionally, you may get benefits like complimentary beverages or a later checkout.

Shop around: You may often find the same hotel room for completely different costs on other booking sites, so check prices with the hotels directly as well as on a few different sites, or comparison sites like Trivago or TripAdvisor.

Hostels

Travelers on a tight budget might consider staying in hostels. They may be a terrific opportunity to meet other tourists since they often feature public spaces, kitchens, and shared rooms.

Many inexpensive hostels can be found in London, making it an excellent choice for those trying to save costs on lodging. Here are several well-known hostels in London along with details on the amenities and services they provide:

YHA London St Pancras: This hostel is located in the vibrant neighborhood of King's Cross, and offers private rooms as well as dormitory-style accommodation. Facilities include a café, bar, and a communal kitchen.

Address: 84-86 Euston Rd, Kings Cross, London N1 9AX, UK

Contact: +44 845 371 9540

Expenses: Prices start at around £20 per night for a dormitory-style room and around £50 per night for a private room.

Generator Hostel London: This stylish hostel is located in the trendy neighborhood of King's Cross, and offers private rooms as well as dormitory-style accommodation. Facilities include a bar, café, and a communal kitchen.

Address: 37 Tavistock Pl, King's Cross, London WC1H 9SE, UK

Contact: +44 20 7380 4040

Expenses: Prices start at around £20 per night for a dormitory-style room and around £50 per night for a private room.

The Capsule & Co. - Hostel: This unique hostel is located in the heart of London, and offers capsule-style accommodation for solo travelers. Facilities include a bar and a communal kitchen.

Address: 8-14 Seagrave Rd, West Brompton, London SW6 1RP, UK

Contact: +44 20 7381 2942

Expenses: Prices start at around £25 per night for a capsule-style room.

Me London Hostel: This modern hostel is located in the heart of London, and offers private rooms as well as dormitory-style accommodation. Facilities include a bar and a communal kitchen.

Address: 336-337 Strand, Covent Garden, London WC2R 1HA, UK

Contact: +44 20 7845 8888

Expenses: Prices start at around £20 per night for a dormitory-style room and around £50 per night for a private room.

Safestay London Elephant & Castle: This hostel is located in the trendy neighborhood of Elephant & Castle, and offers private rooms as well as dormitory-style accommodation. Facilities include a bar, café, and a communal kitchen.

Address: 167-169 Borough High St, London SE1 1NE, UK

Contact: +44 20 7939 9400

Expenses: Prices start at around £20 per night for a dormitory-style room and around £50 per night for a private room.

The Clarendon Hotel: This budget-friendly hotel is located in the heart of London, and offers private rooms as well as dormitory-style accommodation. Facilities include a bar and a communal kitchen.

Address: 28 Craven Rd, Paddington, London W2 3BP, UK

Contact: +44 20 7229 1030

Expenses: Prices start at around £20 per night for a dormitory-style room and around £50 per night for a private room.

The YHA - London Central: This popular hostel is located in the heart of London, and offers private rooms as well as dormitory-style accommodation. Facilities include a bar, café, and a communal kitchen.

Address: 104 Bolsover St, London W1W 5NU, UK

Contact: +44 845 371 9540

Expenses: Prices start at around £20 per night for a dormitory-style room and around £50 per night for a private room.

The Palmers Lodge - Swiss Cottage: This budget-friendly hostel is located in the trendy neighborhood of Swiss Cottage, and offers private rooms as well as dormitory-style accommodation. Facilities include a bar and a communal kitchen.

Address: 36 College Crescent, London NW3 5BJ, UK

Contact: +44 20 7794 7100

Expenses: Prices start at around £20 per night for a dormitory-style room and around £50 per night for a private room.

The YHA - London St Pauls: This popular hostel is located in the heart of London, and offers private rooms as well as dormitory-style accommodation. Facilities include a bar, café, and a communal kitchen.

Address: 356 Goswell Rd, London EC1V 7JQ, UK

Contact: +44 845 371 9540

Expenses: Prices start at around £20 per night for a dormitory-style room and around £50 per night for a private room.

These hostels provide a variety of amenities, and rates might change based on the season and the kind of room you choose. To make sure you choose the ideal hostel for you, it's crucial to compare costs and amenities at several hostels before making a reservation.

These are only a handful of the many hostels that are offered in London; rates and availability may change depending on the season. When making a hostel reservation, be careful to review the specifics of the lodging as well as the amenities and services provided to ensure that they match your requirements.

Serviced apartments

If you want more room and solitude, serviced flats are an excellent choice. They provide greater freedom than hotels and often include a kitchen and living space.

For visitors to London who want more room, privacy, and freedom, serviced flats are a popular option. Here are five of the city's serviced residences:

Cheval Three Quays: This luxury serviced apartment is located in the heart of the city, and offers a range of spacious and well-appointed apartments, many with views of the Tower of London.

Address: 40 Lower Thames St, London EC3R 6AG, UK

Contact: +44 20 7907 0200

Expenses: Prices start at around £150 per night for a studio apartment, and can go up to £500 or more per night for a larger, more luxurious apartment.

The Westbridge Hotel: This serviced apartment hotel is located in the heart of West London, and offers a range of apartments, many with views of the city.

Address: 5-25 Lillie Rd, Fulham, London SW6 1TT, UK

Contact: +44 20 7731 8282

Expenses: Prices start at around £150 per night for a studio apartment, and can go up to £500 or more per night for a larger, more luxurious apartment.

The Strand Palace Hotel: This serviced apartment hotel is located in the heart of London's West End, and offers a range of well-appointed apartments, many with views of the city.

Address: 372 The Strand, London WC2R 0JJ, UK

Contact: +44 20 7845 5000

Expenses: Prices start at around £150 per night for a studio apartment, and can go up to £500 or more per night for a larger, more luxurious apartment.

The Montcalm London: This luxury serviced apartment hotel is located in the heart of the city, and offers a range of spacious and well-appointed apartments, many with views of the city.

Address: 2 Wallenberg Pl, London W1H 7TN, UK

Contact: +44 20 7479 2233

Expenses: Prices start at around £150 per night for a studio apartment, and can go up to £500 or more per night for a larger, more luxurious apartment.

Citadines Trafalgar Square London: This serviced apartment hotel is located in the heart of London's West End, and offers a range of well-appointed apartments, many with views of the city.

Address: 15 Northumberland Ave, Trafalgar Square, London WC2N 5EA, UK

Contact: +44 20 7395 5000

Expenses: Prices start at around £150 per night for a studio apartment, and can go up to £500 or more per night for a larger, more luxurious apartment.

The Good Hotel London: This stylish serviced apartment hotel is located in the heart of London's Royal Docks, and offers a range of well-appointed apartments, many with views of the city.

Address: Royal Victoria Dock, Western Gateway, London, England E16 1AL, UK

Contact: +44 20 7538 8100

Expenses: Prices start at around £100 per night for a studio apartment, and can go up to £400 or more per night for a larger, more luxurious apartment.

The Churchill Hotel: This luxurious serviced apartment hotel is located in the heart of London's West End, and offers a range of spacious and well-appointed apartments, many with views of the city.

Address: 30 Portman Square, London W1H 7BH, UK

Contact: +44 20 7486 8080

Expenses: Prices start at around £150 per night for a studio apartment, and can go up to £500 or more per night for a larger, more luxurious apartment.

The Marylebone Hotel: This stylish serviced apartment hotel is located in the heart of London's Marylebone village, and offers a range of well-appointed apartments, many with views of the city.

Address: 47 Welbeck St, Marylebone, London W1G 8DN, UK

Contact: +44 20 7935 5599

Expenses: Prices start at around £150 per night for a studio apartment, and can go up to £500 or more per night for a larger, more luxurious apartment.

The Royal Garden Hotel: This luxurious serviced apartment hotel is located in the heart of London's Kensington, and offers a range of spacious and well-appointed apartments, many with views of the city.

Address: 2-24 Kensington High St, Kensington, London W8 4PT, UK

Contact: +44 20 7361 3901

Expenses: Prices start at around £150 per night for a studio apartment, and can go up to £500 or more per night for a larger, more luxurious apartment.

The Z Hotel Shoreditch: This stylish serviced apartment hotel is located in the heart of London's trendy Shoreditch neighborhood, and offers a range of well-appointed apartments, many with views of the city.

Address: 65-69 Rivington St, Shoreditch, London EC2A 3AY, UK

Contact: +44 20 7036 0305

Expenses: Prices start at around £100 per night for a studio apartment, and can go up to £400 or more per night for a larger, more luxurious apartment.

Prices for these serviced apartments might change based on the season, the kind of unit you pick, and the location. They provide a variety of services and amenities. Before making a reservation, it's crucial to check costs and amenities across several serviced apartments to be sure you're getting the best deal.

Vacation rentals

Families or groups of friends seeking more room and freedom sometimes opt for vacation rentals such as apartments and homes.

If you want more freedom and space when visiting London, consider renting a vacation home. Here are five of the city's most well-liked vacation rental options:

Airbnb: Airbnb is a website that links visitors with hosts who have places they may rent. In London, there are tens of thousands of holiday rentals on Airbnb, including condos, houses, and even complete mansions.

Address: Since Airbnb has rentals listed all around London, the address may vary depending on the one you choose.

The website address for Airbnb is www.airbnb.com.

Costs: Depending on the size and location of the rental, prices might vary greatly, but you can plan to spend at least £50 per night for a vacation rental in London.

HomeAway: With a large selection of houses available to rent in London, HomeAway is another well-known website for holiday rentals.

Address: Since HomeAway has rentals listed all around London, the address may vary depending on the property you choose.

The website address for HomeAway is www.homeaway.com.

Costs: Depending on the size and location of the rental, prices might vary greatly, but you can plan to spend at least £50 per night for a vacation rental in London.

VRBO: VRBO is a marketplace that focuses on holiday rentals and offers a large number of homes for rent in London.

Address: Since VRBO has rentals listed all throughout London, the address may vary depending on whatever property you choose.

The website address for VRBO is www.vrbo.com.

Costs: Depending on the size and location of the rental, prices might vary greatly, but you can plan to spend at least £50 per night for a vacation rental in London.

TripAdvisor: TripAdvisor is a well-known travel website that has a section for vacation homes. Through TripAdvisor, there are various rental homes in London, including flats, houses, and even full homes.

Address: The address may vary depending on the exact property you pick from TripAdvisor's listings around London.

The website address for TripAdvisor is www.tripadvisor.com.

Costs: Depending on the size and location of the rental, prices might vary greatly, but you can plan to spend at least £50 per night for a vacation rental in London.

Booking.com: Offering a large selection of homes for rent in London, Booking.com is a well-known website for making hotel and vacation rental reservations.

Address: The address may vary depending on the individual rental you pick from Booking.com's listings around London.

Booking.com internet address: www.booking.com

Costs: Depending on the size and location of the rental, prices might vary greatly, but you can plan to spend at least £50 per night for a vacation rental in London.

With your own kitchen and living area, as well as the flexibility to come and go as you choose, vacation rentals may provide a high degree of independence. Before making a reservation, it's important to check pricing and amenities among a range of vacation rental alternatives to be sure you're getting the best deal possible.

Bed and breakfasts Accommodation

Bed and breakfasts: If you're looking for a more intimate and homey experience, bed and breakfasts are a terrific choice. They provide a warm and inviting environment and are often managed by families.

Five B&Bs in London are listed below:

The White House: The White House provides a variety of comfortable and well-appointed rooms, many with views of the city, and is a delightful B&B situated in the center of London's trendy Chelsea area.

Address: 33-35 Eardley Crescent, Chelsea, London SW5 9JE, UK

Contact: +44 20 7370 2394

Expenses: Standard rooms start at around £100 per night, while bigger, more opulent rooms may cost up to or even more than £200 per night.

The London Townhouse: The London Townhouse is a beautiful B&B with a variety of comfortable and well-equipped rooms, many with views of the city, in the center of London's posh Mayfair area.

Address: 26 Upper Grosvenor St, Mayfair, London W1K 7EH, UK

Contact: +44 20 7499 6655

Expenses: Standard rooms start at around £100 per night, while bigger, more opulent rooms may cost up to or even more than £200 per night.

The Kensington House Hotel is a beautiful bed and breakfast located in the renowned Kensington district of London. It offers a selection of appealing and well-appointed rooms, many with views of the city.

Address: 2-6 Courtfield Gardens, Kensington, London SW5 0NP, UK

Contact: +44 20 7244 4885

Expenses: Standard rooms start at around £100 per night, while bigger, more opulent rooms may cost up to or even more than £200 per night.

The Oxford House Hotel: This quaint B&B is situated in the center of London's posh Marylebone district and provides a variety of cozily furnished rooms, several with city views.

Address: 37-39 James St, Marylebone, London W1U 1DX, UK

Contact: +44 20 7935 1866

Expenses: A typical accommodation starts at around £100 per night, while a bigger, more opulent room may cost up to or even more than £200 per night.

Expenses: A typical accommodation starts at around £100 per night, while a bigger, more opulent room may cost up to or even more than £200 per night.

The Rose Garden Bed & Breakfast: The Rose Garden Bed & Breakfast provides a variety of attractive and well-appointed rooms, many of which have views of the city, and is a welcoming B&B situated in the center of London's popular Paddington area.

Address: 34 Sussex Gardens, Paddington, London W2 1UJ, UK

Contact: +44 20 7723 7100

Costs: A typical accommodation starts at around £100 per night, while a bigger, more opulent room may cost up to or even more than £200 per night.

The West End Guesthouse: The West End Guesthouse is a delightful B&B with a variety of comfortable and well-appointed rooms, many with city views, in the center of London's posh Soho area.

Address: 4A New Quebec St, Marylebone, London W1H 7RS, UK

Contact: +44 20 7723 7775

Expenses: Standard rooms start at around £100 per night, while bigger, more opulent rooms may cost up to or even more than £200 per night.

The Bloomsbury House Hotel: The Bloomsbury House Hotel provides a variety of attractive and well-appointed rooms, many with views of the city, and is a delightful B&B in the center of London's trendy Bloomsbury area.

Location: 40 Bedford Pl, Bloomsbury, London, United Kingdom WC1B 5JH

Call (207) 7837 8040.

Expenses: Standard rooms start at around £100 per night, while bigger, more opulent rooms may cost up to or even more than £200 per night.

Whatever your needs or tastes, you're sure to discover the ideal lodging in London. The city has plenty to offer everyone, whether they are searching for a lavish getaway or a more affordable choice.

These B&Bs provide a variety of amenities, and rates might change based on the season, the kind of room you choose, and the location. B&Bs are renowned for their intimate and cozy ambiance and are often managed by families that are enthusiastic about making their visitors feel at home.

Luxury accommodation

Some of the most opulent hotels in the world, complete with top-notch amenities, can be found in London. This kind of lodging is surely something to think about if you want a genuinely opulent experience.

Ten opulent hotels in London are listed below:

The Ritz London: The Ritz London is a renowned luxury hotel in the center of London's West End that provides a variety of accommodation types, many of which have views of Green Park.

Address: 150 Piccadilly, London W1J 9BR, UK

Contact: +44 20 7493 8181

Expenses: Prices start at around £500 per night for a standard room, and can go up to £2,000 or more per night for a suite.

The Mandarin Oriental: This opulent hotel is situated in the heart of London's Knightsbridge district and provides a variety of accommodation sizes and amenities, many of which have views of Hyde Park.

Address: 66 Knightsbridge, London SW1X 7LA, UK

Contact: +44 20 7235 2000

Expenses: Prices start at around £400 per night for a standard room, and can go up to £1,500 or more per night for a suite.

The Four Seasons Hotel London at Park Lane: This luxurious hotel is situated in the center of London's Mayfair area and provides a variety of accommodation sizes and amenities, many of which include views of Hyde Park.

Address: Hamilton Pl, Mayfair, London W1J 7DR, UK

Contact: +44 20 7499 0888

Expenses: Prices start at around £400 per night for a standard room, and can go up to £1,500 or more per night for a suite.

The Dorchester: This luxurious hotel is located in the heart of London's Mayfair neighborhood, and offers a range of spacious and well-appointed rooms and suites, many with views of Hyde Park.

Address: 53 Park Ln, Mayfair, London, W1K 1QA, United Kingdom

Contact: +44 20 7629 8888

Expenses: Prices start at around £400 per night for a standard room, and can go up to £1,500 or more per night for a suite.

The Lanesborough: This luxurious hotel is located in the heart of London's Belgravia neighborhood, and offers a range of spacious and well-appointed rooms and suites, many with views of Hyde Park.

Address: Hyde Park Corner, London, SW1X 7TA, United Kingdom

Contact: +44 20 7259 5599

Expenses: Prices start at around £400 per night for a standard room, and can go up to £1,500 or more per night for a suite.

The Connaught: This luxurious hotel is located in the heart of London's Mayfair neighborhood, and offers a range of spacious and well-appointed rooms and suites, many with views of Mount Street.

Address: Carlos Pl, Mayfair, London, United Kingdom W1B 2AL

Contact: +44 20 7499 7070

Expenses: Prices start at around £400 per night for a standard room, and can go up to £1,500 or more per night for a suite.

The Berkeley: This luxurious hotel is located in the heart of London's Knightsbridge neighborhood, and offers a range of spacious and well-appointed rooms and suites, many with views of Wilton Place.

Address: Wilton Pl, Knightsbridge, London, SW1X 7RL, United Kingdom

Contact: +44 20 7235 6000

Expenses: Prices start at around £400 per night for a standard room, and can go up to £1,500 or more per night for a suite.

The Goring: This luxurious hotel is located in the heart of London's Belgravia neighborhood, and offers a range of spacious and well-appointed rooms and suites, many with views of Beeston Place.

Address: Beeston Pl, Belgravia, London SW1W 0JW, UK

Contact: +44 20 7396 9000

Expenses: Prices start at around £400 per night for a standard room, and can go up to £1,500 or more per night for a suite.

The Savoy: This luxurious hotel is located in the heart of London's Covent Garden neighborhood, and offers a range of spacious and well-appointed rooms and suites, many with views of the River Thames.

Address: Strand, London WC2R 0EU, UK

Contact: +44 20 7845 1400

Expenses: Prices start at around £400 per night for a standard room, and can go up to £1,500 or more per night for a suite.

The Cumberland: This luxurious hotel is located in the heart of London's Oxford Street neighborhood, and offers a range of spacious and well-appointed rooms and suites, many with views of Great Cumberland Place.

Address: Great Cumberland Pl, Marylebone, London W1H 7DL, UK

Contact: +44 20 7724 0000

Expenses: Prices start at around £400 per night for a standard room, and can go up to £1,500 or more per night for a suite.

These luxury hotels offer a range of world-class facilities and services, including spas, restaurants, bars, and fitness centers. They also offer concierge services, 24-hour room service, and other high-end amenities, providing guests with a truly indulgent experience in the heart of London.

However, they can be very expensive, so it's important to consider your budget before making a booking.

Food And Drink

In London

CHAPTER 4: FOOD AND DRINK IN

LONDON

A guide to the city's diverse culinary scene

With a vast variety of foreign cuisines represented in its numerous restaurants and street food carts, London is a city with a vibrant and diversified culinary scene. Following are some pointers for exploring the city's food scene:

Explore different neighborhoods: To obtain a sense of London's eclectic culinary scene, be sure to investigate several neighborhoods, since each has its own distinct culinary personality. For instance, Soho is well-known for its international eateries, while Borough Market is well-known for its street food vendors.

Try traditional British food: The best spot to sample traditional British cuisine is in London, where you can get meals like fish and chips, bangers and mash, and roasted meats. For a genuinely authentic experience, search for real pub-style eateries.

Get a taste of international cuisine: Experiencing ethnic cuisine is recommended since London has a sizable international populace and a diverse culinary scene. The city offers a wide variety of opportunities for experiencing various ethnic cuisines, from Thai and Indian to Turkish and Lebanese.

Don't be hesitant to sample street food: London has a booming street food culture with a variety of cuisine alternatives being offered by several street vendors. Street food is a fantastic chance to experience a variety of meals at a low price, from Ethiopian injera to Indian samosas.

Enjoy afternoon tea: Afternoon tea is a historic British ritual, and you can experience it at many opulent hotels and tea salons in London. Enjoy tea, scones, sandwiches, and pastries in a lovely atmosphere while tasting their subtle tastes.

By using these suggestions, you'll be able to explore London's various culinary attractions and sample the city's varied dining scene.

Recommendations for where to eat and drink in London

One might argue that there has never been a finer moment to explore London, England, via food and drink. In fact, it would be difficult to find anybody who would contest the idea. Right now, The Big Smoke has an embarrassing amount of food and drink options. According to 50 Best, it is home to the top two bars in the whole globe. Additionally, it seems to have major openings every week, bringing variety to one of the most varied eating scenes worldwide.

A comprehensive list of places to visit would have too much information for one article. Instead, I'll give you a practical cross-sampling of where to go and what to buy in the capital city if you find yourself there any time soon.

The Flemings Mayfair: This boutique hotel, the second-oldest in all of London, is bursting at the seams with innovation. A unique "G & Tea Experience" at Manetta's Cocktail Bar combines afternoon tea with botanical-infused tipples, two of the city's most illustrious traditions. For £45 per person, customers may choose one of three gin beverages created with either Whitley Neill Raspberry Gin, Salcombe Gin Rosé, or Nicholson London Dry Gin, along with a variety of freshly baked pastries and bright teas.

One of the most meticulous tasting menus in town is being crafted by head chef Sofian Msetfi at Ormer Mayfair, which is located just next door. The best of British products is used in the five- and eight-course lunch and supper options, with a special emphasis on shellfish and foraged herbs. The area itself has a contemporary elegance that is enhanced by helpful staff and the greatest apéritif cheese cart this side of the English Channel.

The Library Bar at The Lanesborough: This setting is as traditional as it gets for London. Within this five-star Knightsbridge hotel, just off the entrance, is a little bar where the 19th-century cognac stored in lockers next to the bar matches the age of the ancient books on the shelf. Mickael Perron, the bar manager, guides you through a lengthy menu that includes amusing drinks like the Upside Down Fizz, which is served with veggie chips and ginger espuma. The afternoon happy hour's live piano performance contributes to the atmosphere's everlasting transcendence. The hotel is now providing an afternoon tea with a Bridgerton theme that was developed in collaboration with Netflix if you want to appear sophisticated without drinking.

Holy Carrot: a popular vegan restaurant also in Knightsbridge, is attracting customers with its imaginative cuisine that is free of gluten, sugar, preservatives, and chemicals. Given such limitations, it can be difficult to find dishes with robust flavors, but the kitchen succeeds in providing a variety of inventive dishes, such as savory sushi, hearty "Shephard's Pie," and the crowd-pleasing Sexy Tofu, which is the eponymous protein dressed up in red pepper and peanut sauce. The complementary Holy Bar complements that ingenuity by offering a selection of well-balanced drinks with tarot card inspiration. A brand-new Sunday brunch menu aims to satisfy the cravings of vegetarians and vegans for the English custom of protein-heavy weekend roasts.

Berners Tavern is a Fitzrovia institution that serves as both a restaurant and an art gallery. A large selection of meat dishes, such as Côte de Boeuf and slow-roasted lamb shoulder to split, may lead some to believe that this is a contemporary steakhouse. In fact, it wouldn't have any trouble withstanding that kind of verdict. Don't skimp on the seafood however; the appetizer of prawn cocktail with lobster jelly and wasabi puree; the posh fish and chips; and, most significantly, the most opulent lobster mac and cheese you've ever tasted. The drinks are spirit-forward and refreshing. A selection from the mobile champagne cart is an alternative for aperitif drinkers who want something lighter. Jason Atherton, a chef with a Michelin star, is in charge of the kitchen. It made a big splash when it debuted in the London Edition back in 2013, and it still generates plenty of talks today.

Apothecary: This Japanese-inspired restaurant, which bills itself as a "Shoreditch Izakaya," also has a strong reputation for its cocktails. Their Port To The City is a deeper Manhattan prepared with chocolate and coffee, their Zen Garden blends green tea and shiso ingredients into martini territory, and their Tekirawan heated up agave spirit with chile liqueur and yuzu kusho. There is also a tempting selection of spirits and sake available by the glass, as well as by the carafe. Japanese rums and whiskies are particularly prevalent. Sushi hand rolls with fresh crab and flavorful karaage are recommended for the menu. But always keep in mind that the robata is king. Additionally, since it is Shoreditch, live DJ performances fill the area with music on Friday and Saturday nights.

The Walmer Castle is a well-known bar in the center of Notting Hill with a long history that dates back to 1853. Recently, it reopened as a restaurant and whiskey bar in association with The Craigellachie Hotel, one of the most illustrious inns in the scotch nation. The partnership's idea is to provide a little taste of Speyside to London. The transportive effects may be experienced via the consumption of haggis bonbons, Scottish venison carpaccio, and cheeseburgers made with highland beef and Orkney cheese, to name a few. But what's developing in the upper parlor—a single malt shrine coming later this spring—will compel scotch enthusiasts more.

The Twenty Two: Private members' clubs are nothing new in London's Mayfair district. However, the most recent example to appear on the scene in April offers some accessibility without compromising on exceptional elegance. The magnificent 42,500 square-foot building, which is set in an Edwardian mansion with views of Grosvenor Square, is the creation of renowned businessmen Navid Mirtorabi and Jamie Reuben. Underneath a 31-suite luxury hotel, it offers elegant private rooms in addition to an all-day public restaurant, several bars, and a dance club. Executive chef Alan Christie, who oversees the kitchen, offers modern-British cuisine with a Mediterranean flair. Unique liquor bottlings from prominent brands like Patron and The Macallan will be available at the location. The members club will be accessible to those staying on-site.

Shopping
In London

Chapter 5: SHOPPING IN LONDON

Where to find the greatest shopping in town

One of the global centers for shopping is London. You may most likely get it here if you want to. But where can you find the greatest shops in London? We've got you covered, so don't worry.

Megamalls or century-old market customs, designer or antique clothing, jewelry, suits, and foodstuffs. There are definitely more than enough shopping options in London.

However, with so many options, choosing where to buy in London may be challenging.

In response, we are here. The top locations to shop in London are all included in our guide.

Whatever it is that you are looking for can most likely be found right here.

Shopping Locations in London

Portobello Road

Notting Hill

Portobello Road is perhaps the most well-known market in London, and it is a lively bazaar with a lot of singing and dancing going on.

There is little question that antiques and vintage apparel are the primary emphases here; nonetheless, a visit on any day of the week will provide a diverse set of outcomes.

Fruit and vegetables take precedence from Monday through Wednesday. Antiques will be featured on Thursday and Friday. On Saturday, there is a little bit of everything, and on Sunday, there is the vintage clothes market, which is always a big hit.

The problem with Portobello road is that there is so much activity there that there is still enough of everything going on even when one day is intended to be set aside for a certain emphasis area. This is because there is a very high concentration of activities taking place there.

King's Road

Chelsea

If you have money to squander and an eye for brands that are a little bit under the radar, then King's road is definitely for you. It is a hub of fancy boutique boutiques and fine eateries that often attracts the big spenders.

You will be able to discover anything from clothing, shoes, and opticians to home renovations and haircuts – all of which are designer, and which, when combined, makeup to some of the greatest shopping in London.

After being all decked up in that stuff, how about treating yourself to a lunch that will blow your mind? You won't have any problem locating a fine place to eat or drink on King's Road, and the same can be said for the pubs.

Oxford Street

Westminster

Oxford Street, the most renowned shopping district in London and the birthplace of highstreet fashion in the city is where you should go to find the major brands. Oxford Street is home to several of the world's most well-known retail brands' flagship shops, including Adidas, Zara, Accessorize, and Sunglasses Hut, among many others.

There are a number of stores that are examples of this, including Selfridges and John Lewis. As well as being ideal for a little one-stop shopping, with locations to refuel and refresh before rushing back into the battle, these areas are fantastic.

Because of the intense level of competition on Oxford Street, businesses often offer substantial markdowns in the hope of drawing in new clients.

Be prepared to depart with bags in both hands, hanging from your arms, and smothering the poor guy who had no idea what he was getting himself into if this is where you come to buy.

Brick Lane

Aldgate

Brick Alley is widely regarded as one of the city's most desirable locations for vintage shopping. You could easily spend a day browsing the rails of the several antique businesses that line the streets that crisscross this region of East London, yet you still wouldn't have seen all the neighborhood has to offer.

Brick Lane and Shoreditch are often regarded as the hippest neighborhoods in all of London. And as a result, there are a plethora of sites where one may purchase antique items.

However, we will be the first to confess that since there are so many stores, it may be tough to know where to begin. We are fortunate in that we like to think of ourselves as bargain hunters, and as a result, we have spent a significant amount of time perusing the area's antique stores.

What greater motivation could there be to shop in the greatest vintage stores on Brick Lane and Shoreditch if not for the fact that buying used goods is less expensive and healthier for the environment?

Brick Lane and Shoreditch Vintage Shops to Watch Out For

Levisons Vintage Clothing

Levisons specializes in unique vintage apparel and is one of the greatest vintage shopping destinations on Brick Lane. They offer specially chosen, one-of-a-kind men's and women's knitwear, military gear, and unusual workwear.

Since its opening in 2008, Levisons has been a well-liked stop for both collectors and window shoppers. Weekly additions of new merchandise are made, and they are always searching for rare one-of-a-kind products.

Atika London

One of the nicest vintage stores on Brick Lane is Atika London; its enormous size gives you a ton of options. Expect anything from vintage clothing, and lifestyle items, to used home furnishings, all spread out throughout a 2-story Victorian warehouse.

With over 20,000 items of sustainably sourced vintage and remade clothing that have been skillfully picked, Atika is one of the largest vintage boutiques in London. Prices vary, so it's advisable to go downstairs first if you're looking for the greatest deals.

It's difficult to leave a gorgeous store with organized clothing and great music.

Vintage Basement

The fantastic rates at Vintage Basement are why we adore them. There are some great deals to be got here if you're looking for the cheapest vintage stores in Brick Lane.

It's a vintage shopper's heaven as you browse the aisles while dancing to a 90s song. There are many products available for around $10. It's important to go early and return often since the clothing changes frequently.

Serotonin Vintage

You know those unique dream items you still find it hard to believe you got them? That often happens at Serotonin Vintage. Since it opened as a physical location on Brick Lane in 2016, this place has been one of the best thrift stores in Shoreditch.

You'll certainly find what you're looking for, whether it's for a party or simply to freshen up your wardrobe. One of the nicest locations in London to browse for vintage, with wonderfully friendly personnel.

The product is always changing, and while the prices are not the lowest, they are still excellent. London's location for authentic antique treasures.

Bond Street

Mayfair

Since London has been the world's shopping capital for hundreds of years, Bond Street has been the go-to destination for those preoccupied with elegance. If you want anything with a hint of elegance, you should go there.

The 800m-long section of real estate that makes up Bond Street is among the most costly in the world; it is home to Tiffany's, Fenwicks, and Sotheby's. Naturally, there are significant costs associated with buying here.

Along with the majority of other posh brands you can think of, you'll discover shops like Cartier, Louis V, and Hermès as well as a mix of the region's most exclusive custom tailors, cobblers, and galleries.

Even if your pockets aren't deep enough, it's worth a quick look around since it's quite something to behold. Oxford Street is, after all, just around the corner.

Hatton Garden

Holborn

There aren't many locations in London better to go to when you need to get your bling on than Hatton Garden, the diamond capital of the world.

More than 300 jewelry shops can be found along this short length of Holborn, so whether you're searching for a special someone's engagement ring or just want to stand out a bit more, here is undoubtedly the spot to go looking.

You may dine down on a variety of international cuisines at Leather Lane Food Market on Hatton Cross as you decide how much you're ready to spend on the diamond-encrusted dollar-sign necklace you've always wanted.

Westfield Shepherd's Bush

Shepherd's Bush

Even though London has so many unique, specialty shopping options, Westfield must be given credit for what it has accomplished. It really offers everything.

You could shop for anything you need here under the comfort of a single roof, from groceries to new shoes and clothing in brands that you'd need to go a mile for to find together elsewhere.

And you could do it all without ever leaving that exact same roof, with the promise of three delectable meals, coffee breaks, and a movie to liven up your shopping excursion.

Whether for good or bad, it represents enormous American mega-mall materialism at its best. Which one, we'll let you choose.

Camden Market

Camden

Camden Market, a well-liked location for both food and apparel, offers a fantastic selection of everything. This is one of the greatest locations in London to shop due to the variety of goods offered, the cuisine, and the activities.

Here, you may choose from a wide range of apparel alternatives, including antique and hand-made artisanal items. If you look around a little further, you may find some great deals at the neighborhood thrift stores.

But let's face it—the real reason you're here is to indulge in some of Chin Chin Lab's insanely decadent hot chocolate. After a long day of shopping, having that while hanging your feet over the canal is the ideal way to relax.

Bloomsbury

Bloomsbury

The center of the book world, Bloomsbury is home to several outstanding bookstores, ranging in size from little to gigantic.

One of our favorites is Judd Books. They concentrate on the humanities and social sciences, but they also offer a respectable selection of moderately priced books on literature. Check out their simple-to-miss basement area as well.

There are a ton more locations to get items to stock your shelves from if you spend an hour or two browsing around Bloomsbury. And if you're really having trouble finding what you want, it probably can be found in Waterstones on Gower Street, the biggest bookshop in Europe.

Maltby Street

Bermondsey

Maltby Street was just inaugurated in 2010, yet it soon gained popularity as a food and grocery shopping area in London. Probably due to the stunning variety of top-notch produce there.

The majority of the items you purchase here will either be organic or locally or sustainably produced. The vendors at the booths are knowledgeable about their products and eager to address any inquiries you may have.

When you're ready to dine, you may also peruse the restaurants and food vendors, many of which use produce that has just been plucked from the market.

Maltby Street is one of the top shopping districts in London whether you consider yourself a gourmet or just prefer to know where your food comes from.

Carnaby Street

Soho

It would be impossible to discuss shopping in London without mentioning Carnaby Street. There's a reason why it's one of the busiest shopping areas in London.

A variety of fashion labels with a tendency toward a more street-style feel may be found here. There will be both large, recognizable brand shops and smaller boutiques offering a variety of the season's hottest items.

But Carnaby Street's appeal extends beyond its stores. Even if you aren't attempting to buy, it is worthwhile to explore the nearby bars and eateries.

The White Horse is a perfect example of this; it is housed in a stunning Art Deco structure from the 1930s.

Savile Row

Mayfair

Listen up, gentlemen. We should all possess custom-made suits at some time in our lives. The one-size-fits-all outfit that only we can wear.

If you don't already work for the Secret Service, putting it on will get you as near to becoming James Bond as you may get in real life. And I believe that when that moment comes, we will all wish that the suit was made on Savile Row.

With shops from both designer and custom labels, it is essentially the holy zone of suit manufacturers. A couple of the stores cautiously go into the areas of casual clothing and cashmere hoodies.

It costs a lot, as you may anticipate from the best tailors the city has to offer. It's not a terrible location to imagine shopping, though.

Seven Dials

Covent Garden

The way the streets were laid out, all convergent at one point, was really an ingenious way for the city planners to maximize the amount of storefront area (rent was charged per foot of frontage, rather than per square meter back in the 1700s).

Seven Dials was formerly one of London's most hazardous and disreputable neighborhoods, and it served as the model for Hogarth's well-known painting of Gin Lane.

Since then, there has been significant advancement. There is now a wide range of beauticians, top-tier bars and restaurants, flagship fashion boutiques, and boutique apparel.

The greatest location to shop in London, offering a complete shopping experience.

Spitalfields

Tower Hamlets

Since the 1600s, people have traveled to Spitalfields to shop. What do you think of London's retail heritage?

An excursion through contemporary apparel marketplaces and booths offering hand-made jewelry and other souvenirs, such as items to adorn a mantle piece, allows one to follow in their footsteps.

The majority of the clothes are either antique or come from tiny businesses that don't yet have their own physical location. The staff members manning the booths will be delighted to go through the brand's history, ideas, and aspirations.

Spitalfields market is the place to go if you, like us, prefer to know where the products you purchase originate from or have a deeper relationship to a piece of apparel than "I bought it from (insert random high-street fashion name here)"

We don't think the culinary alternatives will disappoint you either.

Tips for finding unique and authentic souvenirs

London is a city with a rich history and cultural legacy, and you may bring home a variety of original and genuine souvenirs to remember your trip. Here are some pointers for selecting the top mementos:

Visit local markets: You may discover a broad range of one-of-a-kind and handcrafted products at London's thriving markets, including Camden Market, Portobello Road Market, and Borough Market, including apparel, jewelry, and home goods.

Local markets in London are a terrific location to buy one-of-a-kind, genuine gifts that you won't find in standard tourist stores. Here are some suggestions to maximize your market buying experience:

Arrive Early: To avoid crowds and improve your shopping experience, aim to arrive early in the morning at many of London's markets.

Do Your Research: Find out which marketplaces offer the kinds of goods you're interested in by doing some research prior to your trip. For instance, Borough Market is well-known for its food booths, while Camden Market is well-known for its alternative clothing and jewelry.

Bargain: Most market sellers are amenable to price negotiations, so don't be shy about doing so. Being kind and considerate might help you negotiate a better price.

Try Street Food: While you're in the market, take advantage of the chance to sample some of the regional street food. You may choose from a broad range of delectable goodies, including unique foreign cuisines and classic British foods.

Support Local Artisans: By purchasing souvenirs from neighborhood markets, you'll be supporting small businesses and local craftsmen. A genuinely unique and one-of-a-kind souvenir of your vacation to London will also be yours to keep.

Explore independent shops: The city is teeming with small stores that sell a variety of one-of-a-kind things, including vintage clothes, books, and artisanal goods, in areas like Shoreditch, Covent Garden, and Brick Lane.

You'll have the chance to support regional companies and artists by shopping at small boutiques, where you may also discover genuinely unique goods. You're likely to discover something that strikes your attention, whether you're shopping for handcrafted jewelry, antique apparel, or unusual home products.

The ceramics business The Peanut Vendor in Notting Hill, the vintage clothes shop Beyond Retro in Shoreditch, and the jewelry store The Hour in Soho are a few independent shops in London that are worth visiting. Whether you're buying for yourself or other people, these businesses provide a vast selection of goods, so you're likely to discover something you enjoy.

It's a good idea to visit small shops with an open mind and be prepared to browse for a while. Take the time to talk with the proprietors and learn about the items and their history since shopping at these places is often more intimate and engaging. You'll never know what unusual findings you'll make!

Look for British-made products: Look for products that are manufactured in Britain, such as tweed clothing, pottery, and regional delicacies, if you want mementos that are really symbolic of the nation.

A terrific way to carry a bit of Britain home with you is to purchase British-made goods. These items are often of great quality and provide a distinctive picture of British culture and history. For instance, tweed cloth, a traditional material connected to Scotland, is used to create products like scarves, hats, and coats. Another well-liked option for a British-made souvenir is pottery, with classic pieces often showcasing distinctive patterns and themes like the Union Jack. Another well-liked choice for a British-made memento is traditional sweets like fudge and shortbread, which come in a range of flavors and packaging choices. Look for things that have been created in Britain and have the proper labeling when purchasing British-made goods to verify authenticity.

Consider traditional British items: Teapots, postcards, and other traditional British mementos may make wonderful presents and serve as a remembrance of your journey.

Teapots, postcards, and mugs are all classic British keepsakes that are a wonderful way to remember your visit to London. These goods are offered by street vendors and souvenir stores all around the city. Additionally, you may choose more distinctive handmade goods like hand-embroidered clothing or hand-painted pottery, which are often available at regional markets. It's usually a good idea to search for products that are created in Britain and have classic motifs, like the Union Jack or royal crests, when purchasing these kinds of souvenirs. You may be certain that you are bringing a genuine piece of British culture home in this manner. Additionally, be careful to confirm that the item you're interested in is a real one and not a subpar copy.

Buy at museum shops: London's museums are a terrific location to buy one-of-a-kind and culturally relevant souvenirs since many of them have shops where they offer goods associated with their exhibits, such as prints, books, and jewelry.

A great spot to discover one-of-a-kind and historically important souvenirs is in museum stores. They provide a large selection of goods, including prints, books, jewelry, and other items, that are connected to the exhibits on show at the museum. Many of London's well-known museums, including the British Museum, the National Gallery, and the Tate Modern, include gift stores. These stores often provide unique presents that cannot be found anywhere else since they sell goods that are specifically created for the museum. Additionally, many of the things in museum stores are produced locally, allowing you to support local industry and take a bit of London with you. Simply look on the website of your preferred museum for information on where to locate museum stores in London, or ask a museum staff member while you are there.

You should be able to acquire a range of one-of-a-kind and genuine mementos to bring home from your trip to London by using these suggestions.

Arts And Culture

In

London

CHAPTER 6: ARTS AND CULTURE IN

LONDON

The best museums, galleries, and cultural events in the city

London doesn't mess around when it comes to amazing museums; the city is home to over 130 fantastic museums that appeal to all interests and curiosities.

Therefore, you can be sure to find the ideal museum in London whether you want to learn more about the history of the Second World War, uncover priceless Islamic and Asian art, or gaze in awe at stunning modern artworks.

Here is a list of the top 14 museums in London that are well worth seeing. You may see works of art and antiques of the highest caliber without breaking the bank since the majority of them don't charge admission!

The Top 14 London Museums

Natural History Museum

The finest fun will be had by science enthusiasts when seeing the Natural History Museum in London. This top-notch museum, which is situated in the South Kensington neighborhood, is home to a stunning collection of 80 million artifacts that date back billions of years.

The enormous blue whale skeleton in Hintze Hall, the fossils in the renowned Dinosaurs display, and meteorites from space are just a few of the highlights of the Natural History Museum's collection.

Hours of Operation: 10 a.m. to 5 p.m., Monday through Sunday; closed December 24–26.

Address: Cromwell Road in South Kensington

Science Museum

For interested tourists hoping to learn more about the inventions that helped create the modern world, the Science Museum is another important place to go. The museum, which was founded in 1857, is a significant institution and one of London's top tourist destinations, with over 1 million people a year.

Visitors may browse the two buildings of the museum and find a variety of priceless works of scientific progress. These include a Pilot ACE computer from 1950, Helen Sharman's Space Suit, which was created in 1991, and the Wells Cathedral Clock, one of the oldest clocks ever made.

Daily hours of operation are 10 am to 6 pm.

Address: South Kensington's Exhibition Road

British Museum

The British Museum, which was established in 1753, was the first national museum to include all branches of knowledge. Visitors will be pleasantly delighted to discover an impressive permanent collection there that includes eight million items that span two million years of human history and culture.

Explore the vast halls of the museum to be amazed by renowned artifacts like the Rosetta Stone, an Egyptian mummy, and Parthenon sculptures. The Rosetta Stone is a dark-colored granodiorite stela that was cut during the Hellenistic period.

Every day from 10 a.m. to 5 p.m.

Great Russell Street is the address.

London Transport Museum

Do you want to know more about the interesting connection between transportation and London's expansion? The Transport Museum should therefore definitely be visited. There, you'll find more than 500,000 items, including more than 80 classic cars from 200 years of London's history. Among the museum's treasures are an 1890s-era railway carriage called the padded cell and the red Routemaster bus, which was the world's first underground steam train.

Hours of Operation: Daily 10 am to 6 pm

Covent Garden Piazza is the address.

Victoria and Albert Museum

The biggest museum dedicated to ornamental, applied, and design arts is located in London. A permanent collection of more than 2.27 million items, ranging from ancient Chinese pottery to evening gowns by Alexander McQueen, is housed at this adored institution.

The Victoria and Albert Museum's highlights include Raphael's paintings, Auguste Rodin's sculptures, and Queen Victoria's sparkling sapphire and diamond coronet.

Daily hours are 10 a.m. to 5 p.m.; on Friday, they are 10 a.m. to 22 p.m.

Postal Code: Cromwell Road

National Gallery

One of the most magnificent museums in the whole world is London's National Gallery. This distinguished institution, which is tucked away in the center of Trafalgar Square, is home to a priceless collection of over 2,300 works of art by notable painters including Leonardo da Vinci, Vincent van Gogh, Diego Velázquez, Sandro Botticelli, and Johannes Vermeer.

Van Gogh's Sunflowers, Claude Monet's Water Lily Pond, and Jan van Eyck's "The Arnolfini Portrait" are just a few of the outstanding masterpieces you'll have the opportunity to view at the National Gallery.

Open every day from 10 am to 6 pm, and on Friday until 9 pm.

Address: Trafalgar Square

Imperial War Museum

The Imperial War Museum in London, which is housed in a former hospital, was established to preserve the exceptional experiences of those who were involved in World Wars I and II.

Visitors may find exhibits of military vehicles, aircraft, and equipment, as well as archives of personal and government papers, pictures, oral history recordings, and recordings from the museum's award-winning galleries.

Two enormous naval cannons constructed for two distinct British navy ships during the First World War, a charging Russian T34 tank, and the Spitfire—one of the most renowned fighter planes of World War II—are some of the highlights of the museum.

Hours of Operation: Daily 10 AM to 6 PM

Address: Lambeth Road

Fashion and Textile Museum

The only museum in the UK that exclusively displays modern fashion and textile design is the Fashion and Textile Museum. The museum, which was established by the British designer Zandra Rhodes, doesn't have a permanent collection; instead, it regularly offers vibrant temporary exhibits with well-known creatives from all over the globe.

The museum will host an exhibition that examines the captivating textile patterns created by Andy Warhol, a well-known and important pop artist, from March 31 to September 10, 2023. a must-see!

Tuesday through Saturday, 11 a.m. to 6 p.m.

Address: 83 Bermondsey Street

Design Museum

The Design Museum is the top museum in the world dedicated to modern design in all its forms. It was founded by Sir Terence Conran in 1989 and moved to Kensington in 2016.

The museum is housed in a refurbished facility that was once used by the Commonwealth Institute and has a top-notch collection of more than 3000 items. These artifacts cover all facets of design, including architecture, fashion, furniture, product and graphic design, digital media, and transportation, and range from the first manifestations of modernism in the early 1900s to the most cutting-edge examples of the current design.

The museum offers two locations for amazing temporary exhibits in addition to one presentation of the permanent collection. "Ai Weiwei: Making Sense," the artist's first show concentrating on design, will be on display at the Design Museum from July 1 through July 30, 2023.

Sunday through Thursday, 10 a.m. to 6 p.m., and Friday and Saturday, 10 a.m. to 9 p.m.

The location is 224–238 Kensington High Street.

Royal Air Force Museum

The Royal Air Force Museum (RAF), which encompasses five buildings and hangars depicting the history of aviation and the Royal Air Force, is beautifully situated inside the old Hendon Aerodrome.

The museum is home to around 1.3 million artifacts that trace the development of the British air and space force, which was established on 1 April 1918, at the close of the First World War.

You may see the Westland Sea King helicopter and the genuine Avro Lancaster S-Sugar fighter plane from the Battle of Britain while touring the museum.

Every day from 10 a.m. to 5 p.m.

Address: Grahame Park Way

Sir John Soane's Museum

The old residence of neo-classical architect and voracious book collector John Soane is now home to Sir John Soane's Museum.

You may find a sparkling collection of artifacts, furniture, sculptures, architectural models, and jaw-dropping paintings by artists like Hogarth, Turner, and Canaletto while touring Soane's amazing home.

Additionally, the Research Library has 30,000 architectural drawings that may be seen by appointment.

Hours of Operation: Wednesday through Sunday, 10 am to 5 pm

Address: 13 Lincoln's Inn Fields

Tate Modern

One of the biggest museums of modern and contemporary art in the world is Tate Modern. The museum has a staggering collection of works by artists including Salvador Dali, Auguste Rodin, Pablo Picasso, and Andy Warhol, covering a total interior floor space of 371,350 square feet.

Be sure to see the famed "Marilyn Diptych" artwork by Andy Warhol, "Nude Woman With Necklace" by Pablo Picasso, and "Seagram Murals" by Mark Rothko while touring the museum's permanent galleries.

Monday through Sunday, 10 a.m. to 6 a.m.

Address: Bankside

Charles Dickens Museum

Greetings from one of London's most intriguing locations. The museum is situated at 48 Doughty Street, where Dickens lived in London from 1837 to 1839 and penned Oliver Twist.

Visitors will get the opportunity to learn about one of England's most well-known and beloved authors in this pretty typical middle-class Victorian house, which has been furnished as if Dickens himself had just gone.

A painting of Charles Dickens by R. W. Buss titled Dickens' Dream, multiple first editions, original manuscripts, authentic letters by Dickens, and several personal objects held by Dickens and his family are among the priceless artifacts housed in the museum.

The museum also has Dickens' only surviving article of clothes on exhibit.

Tuesday through Sunday, 10 a.m. to 5 p.m.

Address: 48-49 Doughty Street

Horniman Museum and Gardens

In Forest Hill, South London, there lies the magnificent and welcoming Horniman Museum and Gardens. The museum, which has been there since the Victorian era, has an impressive collection of almost 350,000 items spanning natural history, cultural relics, and musical instruments.

There, visitors will find 80,000 items from all over the globe, a sizable collection of taxidermied animals, some 4,700 butterflies, and a pair of bone clappers fashioned in Egypt about 3,500 years ago that resemble human hands.

Hours of Operation: Daily 10 am to 5:30 pm

Address: Forest Hill, 100 London Road

FAQ

Are London's museums worth visiting?

Yes. The museums in London are among the best in the world, and they often offer excellent exhibits on a variety of subjects, from contemporary art to history and fashion.

What are London's top museums?

London's top museums are:

- Natural History Museum;
- Science Museum;
- British Museum;
- London Transport Museum;

- Victoria and Albert Museum;

- National Gallery;

- Imperial War Museum;

- Fashion and Textile Museum;

- Design Museum;

- Royal Air Force Museum;

- Sir John Soane's Museum;

- Tate Modern;

- Charles Dickens Museum;

- Horniman Museum and Gardens.

Are London's museums free?

Yes. There is no admission price for the majority of London's top museums, including the British Museum, National Gallery, and Tate Britain.

London's most popular cultural events

London is a city that hosts many cultural events throughout the year, including a wide variety of exhibits, concerts, theatrical plays, and festivals. Whether you like theater, contemporary art, or classical music, there is bound to be something that piques your interest.

In London, some of the most well-liked cultural events are:

The London Film Festival: The London Film Festival, which is held in October, features new and highly acclaimed films as well as the greatest in international and British cinema.

One of the biggest and most renowned film festivals in the world is the London Film Festival. Since its founding in 1957, it has always taken place in October. With a particular emphasis on British and international cinema, the festival presents a broad selection of films from throughout the globe, including recent releases and highly renowned productions.

Over the course of two weeks, the festival hosts a range of activities, such as film screenings, filmmaker Q&A sessions, and industry events for experts. The festival draws a broad crowd of moviegoers, filmmakers, and business people and is a unique chance to see the finest in both modern and vintage cinema.

The London Film Festival offers a variety of special events in addition to its regular program, including gala screenings of the year's top movies, award ceremonies, and roundtable conversations with industry professionals. The London Film Festival is certainly worth checking out, whether you're a die-hard movie fan or simply seeking a good time and a cultural education.

The London Literature Festival: This yearly festival, which takes place in the summer, offers a variety of performances, seminars, and debates with some of the best authors in the world.

The London Literature Festival honors the written word in a dynamic and captivating way. This festival, which takes place over a number of weeks every summer, is a special chance for readers to discover the impact of literature in various formats.

The festival offers a wide variety of performances, conversations, and workshops with some of the best authors in the world. Attending events centered on poetry, children's literature, non-fiction, and fiction allows participants to interact with authors from across the globe who are pushing the frontiers of the written word.

The festival offers guests the opportunity to learn about fresh viewpoints and views in addition to activities that include well-known authors. Additionally, there are occasions that honor the craft of storytelling, including live readings, slam poetry performances, and storytelling workshops.

Libraries, theaters, and cultural institutions are just a few of the locations where the event is hosted around the city. The festival is accessible to individuals of all ages and backgrounds since a large number of the activities are free and open to the public. The London Literature Festival is a must-attend event for anybody who values the power of the written word, regardless of whether you've always been a book lover or are just searching for a rich cultural experience.

London Fashion Week: This event, one of the greatest in the world for fashion, occurs twice a year, often in February and September. It displays the most recent collections from some of the most renowned fashion designers in the world.

Celebrities, reporters, and members of the fashion business from all over the globe attend the much anticipated London Fashion Week. The exhibition features the most recent collections from a variety of fashion designers, both well-known figures and up-and-coming artists. In a series of runway shows, conferences, and events throughout the week, designers showcase their collections, giving spectators an early peek at the newest trends in clothing.

Several sites in the city, including well-known ones like Brewer Street Car Park, The Store Studios, as well as the National History Museum, host London Fashion Week. The week includes a variety of activities in addition to the runway shows, providing guests an opportunity to network, mingle, and interact with the fashion industry. These events include exhibits, seminars, and parties.

If you're planning to attend London Fashion Week, be advised that it might be challenging to get tickets since the event is very elite and by invitation only. Attending exhibits, performances, and other activities that are free and open to the public will still allow you to take in the thrill of the week.

Notting Hill Carnival: The biggest street festival in Europe, this annual celebration takes place during the August Bank Holiday weekend. A colorful procession of music, dancing, and costumes, as well as food booths and other entertainment, are all part of the carnival.

A significant occasion in London's calendar, the Notting Hill Carnival is a lively celebration of Caribbean culture. Every year during the August Bank Holiday weekend, the event draws hundreds of thousands of tourists from all over the globe.

The carnival procession, which features people dancing to the rhythm of steel drums and other music while wearing bright costumes, is the centerpiece of the celebration. Caribbean food vendors, live music stages, sound systems, and various types of entertainment may be found throughout the parade route.

Over the course of the weekend, there will be a plethora of additional events in addition to the march, such as seminars, community gatherings, and parties. The Notting Hill Carnival is an event not to be missed, whether you're into music, dancing, or simply taking in the ambiance.

The festival's precise dates vary from year to year, but it always falls on the August Bank Holiday weekend, which is the final weekend in August. As the carnival is quite popular and many hotels as well as other accommodations in the region tend to fill up fast, it is advisable to plan ahead and reserve your lodgings well in advance if you want to enjoy the carnival to the fullest.

The National Theatre: The National Theatre, one of the most prominent theater organizations in the UK, presents a variety of shows all year long, including both classic plays and modern pieces.

One of London's top theatrical venues, the National Theatre is renowned for its cutting-edge shows and dedication to supporting emerging artists. It is situated close to the London Eye and other well-known sites on the South Bank of the River Thames. The theater presents a variety of shows all year long, including classic plays, modern plays, musicals, and new works. The National Theatre is an excellent venue to introduce kids to the theater since it also offers a schedule of seminars and other activities for young people.

Tickets for performances at the National Theatre may be bought in advance or on the day of the event. Prices vary based on the performance and the seat, however, discounts for students, the elderly, and other organizations are often offered. There are numerous local bus and rail stops, making it simple to take public transportation to get to the theater. It's a terrific spot to spend an evening in London since there are several pubs and eateries around.

The Royal Opera House: Fans of classical music and dance must go to the Royal Opera House, which is the home of the Royal Opera and the Royal Ballet.

One of London's most famous cultural centers and a top attraction for fans of classical music and dance is the Royal Opera House. It was founded in 1732 and has a long history, hosting a number of internationally known performers throughout the years. Two of the top performing arts organizations in the world today call it home: the Royal Opera and the Royal Ballet.

Classical ballets, operas, and concerts are just a few of the acts that are available at the Royal Opera House. Audiences will have a memorable experience in its spectacular theater, which has amazing acoustics and lavish decor. Along with several exhibits and displays that highlight its extensive history, the Royal Opera House also includes a well-stocked gift store for anyone searching for a memento.

The Royal Opera House offers guided tours that give guests a behind-the-scenes peek at the building and a fascinating window into the world of classical music and ballet. These tours are a great chance to get a behind-the-scenes look at one of London's most significant cultural institutions since they often include stops at the stage, the costume departments, and the rehearsal rooms.

The Royal Opera House is readily accessible by public transportation since it is situated in Covent Garden, the center of London, and is close to multiple subway stations, including Covent Garden and Charing Cross. Anyone interested in classical dance and music in London must pay a visit to the Royal Opera House because of its top-notch performances, extensive history, and breathtaking location.

The Barbican Centre: One of London's top cultural organizations, this multi-arts space presents a wide variety of exhibits, concerts, and plays all year long.

In the core of London's Barbican Estate stands the Barbican Centre, a famous cultural hub. Since its 1982 debut, it has developed into the center of the city's cultural life, hosting a wide variety of exhibits, concerts, and plays in its several theaters, galleries, and cinemas. The Barbican Art Gallery, the Barbican Library, and the London Symphony Orchestra are also housed there.

The Barbican Centre is known for putting on cutting-edge and provocative events that highlight the greatest in modern art, music, theater, and cinema. The Barbican Center has something for everyone, from classical music concerts to cutting-edge exhibits and thought-provoking plays. The center is renowned for its beautiful architecture and design, a modernist marvel made of concrete, glass, and steel, in addition to its cultural activities.

Aside from its many other amenities, the Barbican Centre offers visitors access to a number of food establishments, a sizable park and courtyard, and a cutting-edge theater complex. Anyone interested in London's arts and culture, whether they are from the city or are simply passing through, must visit the Barbican Centre.

West End Theater: The Royal Opera House, the National Theatre, as well as the Globe Theatre, are just a few of the world's most renowned theaters that can be found in London's West End. There is something for everyone among the many shows offered.

One of the most well-liked cultural attractions in London is the West End theatrical scene, which is well-known across the globe. The West End provides a wide variety of performances to suit all tastes, from enduring musicals like "Les Misérables" and "The Phantom of the Opera" to timeless classics like "Hamlet" and "Romeo and Juliet." The theaters themselves often have elaborate architecture, opulent interiors, and cutting-edge amenities that are just as remarkable as the performances they host.

It is possible for visitors to the West End to buy tickets in advance or on the day of the performance, however, it is generally recommended to do so, particularly for popular productions. Additionally, there are many ticket brokers that provide specials and discounts, so it pays to shop around before you attend.

Along with the major shows, the West End also offers a variety of unique occasions and seasons, such as Shakespeare in the West End, which takes place every summer and brings the plays of the Bard to some of the best theaters in the area.

Any traveler to London must experience a trip to the West End theater, which is a memorable and delightful experience.

Music Festivals: Numerous music events, including the renowned Glastonbury Festival, the Reading and Leeds Festivals, and the Wireless Festival, are held throughout the year in London. These occasions provide a wonderful chance to watch both well-known and emerging performers.

Hip hop, electronic dance music, indie rock, and other genres are all represented in the London music festivals (EDM). In different parts of the city, such as parks, outdoor arenas, and inside venues, they are held. For instance, Glastonbury, one of the biggest music festivals in the world, draws over 200,000 visitors annually to Worthy Farm, Somerset. Over the August Bank Holiday weekend, the Reading and Leeds Festivals draw some of the greatest names in rock, indie, and alternative music. The Wireless Festival is an urban music event that takes place over multiple days and is dedicated to hip hop, grime, and R&B. The festival is held at Finsbury Park.

Visitors may enjoy a variety of music, cuisine, and entertainment choices at music festivals in London, which provide a special and unforgettable experience. They are a fantastic opportunity to see the city's music scene and take advantage of the warm weather. Planning ahead is necessary, however, since these popular events may cause tickets to sell out rapidly and lodging options to become scarce.

Art Exhibitions: London is well known for having a strong art scene, and the city is home to several galleries and museums where you can see exhibits of the work of both local and foreign artists. The National Gallery, Tate Modern, and Saatchi Gallery are some of the city's most well-known attractions.

Anyone interested in modern and classical art must attend the London art shows. There is something for everyone, from digital art to painting and sculpture. The National Gallery, Tate Modern, and Saatchi Gallery host some of the largest exhibits in the city. With exhibits exhibiting works by artists like Vincent van Gogh, Pablo

Picasso, and Banksy, among others, these institutions are known for displaying the finest in local and international talent.

The National Gallery features works by some of the most well-known painters in history, including Rembrandt, Botticelli, and Leonardo da Vinci. The Tate Modern, on the other hand, specializes in modern and contemporary art and hosts exhibits that include pieces by some of the most creative and important painters in the world, including Matisse, Warhol, and Rothko.

The Saatchi Gallery, in Chelsea, is a prominent venue for contemporary art, hosting exhibits of pieces by both well-known artists and some of the most intriguing up-and-coming talent in the world. The gallery is renowned for its avant-garde shows, many of which focus on fresh and developing art forms including Pop Art and Street Art.

The art exhibits in London are not to be missed, whether you are an art enthusiast or just want to learn more about the city's cultural landscape. There will undoubtedly be one exhibition that appeals to everyone given the abundance of top-tier universities available.

These cultural events provide a wonderful chance to experience some of the finest that London has to offer, whether you are a native or a tourist to the city.

Recommendations for experiencing London's creative side

There are numerous ways to see London's creative side. The city has a rich cultural legacy. Here are some suggestions:

Visit the West End: The theater district in London's West End is home to many of the most well-known plays and musicals in the world. The most well-liked productions are "Hamilton," "Wicked," and "The Lion King."

Explore the galleries: London is home to a bustling contemporary art scene, with a wide variety of galleries and institutions displaying the creations of both national and international artists. A few of the numerous places worth seeing are the National Gallery, the Saatchi Gallery, and the Tate Modern.

Attend a live performance: London has much to offer performers of all stripes, whether they like plays, concerts, or dance shows. Amazing live performances may be found at places like the Royal Albert Hall, Barbican Center, and Roundhouse.

Take a street art tour: Many of the walls and buildings in London are covered with spectacular murals and graffiti, and the city is well-recognized for its street art movement. You may either go on your own exploration or join a guided street art tour to view some of the greatest works.

Visit the design museums: The Victoria and Albert Museum and Design Museum are two of the many design-focused museums located in London. The most cutting-edge designs in furniture, clothing, architecture, and technology are shown at these museums.

Outdoor Activities In London

CHAPTER 7: OUTDOOR ACTIVITIES

IN LONDON

Parks and green spaces to explore in the city

London is renowned for having a large number of lovely parks and green areas, which provide a welcome respite from the busy metropolis. Here are a few of the most well-known parks to visit:

1. Richmond Park

The 1,012 hectares of forest, grassland, and parkland of Richmond Park, one of London's eight royal parks, are crisscrossed with pathways and ponds, making it the ideal area to get lost in.

The park is home to a variety of animals, including 630 red and fallow deer that have been roaming freely there since 1637. It is also home to 144 different bird species, including swans, bluetits, and white-headed Eurasian coots, as well as rabbits, foxes, and bats. Don't miss the Isabella Plantation in the southern part of the park, which is in full bloom with golden narcissi, camellias, and magnolias.

Make a pit break at the cafe at Petersham Nurseries outside the park's northwestern boundary before continuing on the trail along the River Thames to Ham House and Garden for an all-day stroll. The estate from the 17th century was created by a Charles I of England acquaintance. You may tour its gardens if you make reservations.

2. Bushy Park

Behind Hampton Court Palace in Hampton, close to Richmond, lies Bushy Park, another royal park. The area, which was formerly King Henry VIII's hunting field, has subsequently housed the Ministry of Defence during the Cold War, a hospital for Canadian soldiers in World War I, a US air base in World War II, and a hospital for Canadian soldiers.

It may be paired with a lengthy walk from Richmond and is located just off the River Thames. Although the 445-hectare area is less well-known than Richmond Park, 320 red and fallow deer call it home. A wonderful (and terrifying) sight is watching stags and bucks fight for females during the mating season in the fall.

The park is essentially split in half by Sir Christopher Wren's mile-long Chestnut Avenue. Follow the Longford River south from the Diana Fountain to the Upper Lodge Water Gardens, which is a section of a historic canal. Watch out for kestrel, kingfisher, and woodpecker.

3. Holland Park

What's remained of the estate of a private mansion built in the early seventeenth century is this park in Kensington, close to the Design Museum. After strolling through the park's formal gardens, do a circle via the northern forest. You may enter Kyoto Garden by following the route as it is around the grounds.

The serene Japanese-style garden has a multi-tiered waterfall that empties into a carp-filled pond. The scene, which resembles a Japanese postcard, is completed with stone lanterns and maple trees. Watch out for peacocks strutting freely over the grounds and squirrels dashing between stepping stones to display their plumage.

4. Hampstead Heath

Explore Hampstead Heath in Hampstead if walking in mud while wearing wellies is your idea of fun. The 320-hectare woods provided the monarch with game and London with water during the reign of King Henry VIII. It became a popular area for amusement when a railroad station opened there in 1860, and it has remained so ever since.

Highlights include Parliament Hill, a 98-meter hill with views of St. Paul's Cathedral and The Shard, a lovely pergola, and the English Heritage site Kenwood. Also on the heath are 18 ponds. There are three of them in the east, one for each sex, so fans of wild swimming may take a dip there.

Here, too, birders are in luck. Watch for wagtails along the lake in the summer and wheatear and whinchat in the meadows in the fall. Watch out for bluetits, greenfinches, and the occasional parakeet in the woods.

5. Trent Country Park

The Cockfosters tube in Enfield is just a minute's walk away, yet many Londoners have never ever heard of this park. The park was noted in William the Conqueror's Domesday Book, which was completed in 1086. After Henry VIII, Elizabeth I, and James I used it for hunting, George III's doctor received it as a gift.

Visitors might get lost in the 167-hectare area, which is larger than the capital's Regent's Park. A 3.8km walk leads you through the nicest areas, which include lakes, meadows, and woods in addition to an avenue of lime trees outside the main gate. Watch out for sycamore and oak trees where muntjac deer, partridge, and pheasants may be hiding.

At sunset, you could also see rabbits, while foxes and bats emerge at night. Bringing your binoculars will be worthwhile since you could see great spotted woodpeckers, kestrels, goldfinches, and coral-chested chaffinches as well.

6. Walthamstow Wetlands

Less than five minutes walk separates this wildlife reserve from Tottenham Hale tube station, which is inaugurated in 2017. Over three million people get water from the site's ten reservoirs.

The grounds' center is traversed by a small bicycle path. Don't miss the observation platform in the Grade II-listed Coppermill Tower. You may continue the same trail or circle the reservoirs on pedestrian-only pathways. Rainbow trout, carp, bream, eel, pike, and perch may all be caught by anglers with a license. Twitchers may hide out in the meanwhile.

In the spring, you may see woodcocks and oystercatchers; in the summer, you might see long-tailed ducks, peregrine falcons, and red-crested pochards; and in the fall, you might see uncommon species like the green sandpiper. Rose-chested bullfinch, siskin, and firecrest—named for their fiery red strip of hair—are attracted to wintertime habitats. Kingfishers may be spotted all year round.

7. Lea Valley

In east London's Lea Valley, the River Lea flows. From Walthamstow Wetlands, ride a Santander Cycles or electric Lime bike south to Springfield Park. Hackney Marshes, often known as the Hackney Riviera, may be reached by crossing the river and continuing on the path via Lea Valley Marina.

Even though it's not on the Côte d'Azur, the wooded walk that follows the river is a lovely, undiscovered location that evokes Kent in Britain rather than London. Before arriving at Queen Elizabeth Olympic Park at the entrance of the River Thames, you'll cross cattle and horses grazing in rolling meadows as the sun breaks through the tunnel of mature trees.

8. Regent's Canal

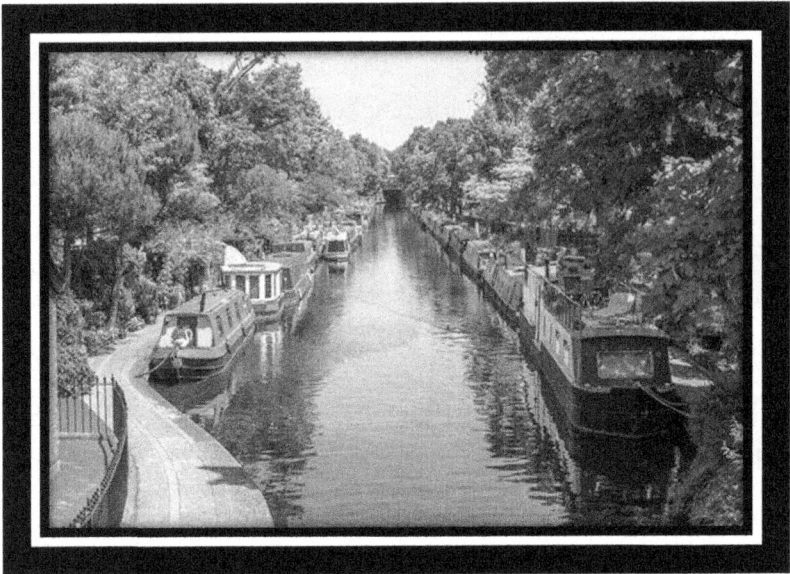

The Regent's Canal, built by the same architect who built Buckingham Palace, connected the Grand Union Canal in west London to the River Thames in the east of the city when it was opened in 1816.

Although fairly metropolitan, the area between Limehouse and Angel is not without its beauty. Although cyclists are welcome, walkers have the right of way on the constrained towpath that runs beside Broadway Market, London Fields, and many locks.

Once you get to Victoria Park, go around the Chinese pagoda in the center of the boating lake and then check out the ancient English garden, East Lake, and model boating lake. To the south, Mile End

Park and Limehouse Basin are also accessible. The basin is connected to the River Lea and Queen Elizabeth Olympic Park via the Limehouse Cut towpath.

9. Hainault Forest Country Park

Hainault Forest Country Park is all that is left of the Forest of Essex, which served as a royal hunting preserve in the 12th century. The 113-hectare estate is near Redbridge, in the northeastern part of London.

The London Loop route runs around the center of the park, through a boating lake and through grassland and forest made primarily of poplar, oak, and ash trees, as well as horseback riding and cycling trails. Although it's presently closed, you may be able to visit Foxburrows Farm, which is home to farm animals, exotic birds, and meerkats.

Birdwatchers may recognize the sound of a nightingale or a rare turtle dove in the summer, while the orange-breasted brambling from Scandinavia may be heard in the winter. Along with badgers and bank voles, the park is also home to several kinds of bats and butterflies.

Recommendations for outdoor adventures and activities

With a variety of parks and green areas, as well as chances for activities like hiking, cycling, and water sports, London is a terrific location for outdoor lovers. Here are some suggestions for outdoor excursions and sports in the city:

Hiking at the Heath: One of London's biggest parks, Hampstead Heath is a wonderful area to go for a stroll or a walk. Over 800 acres of hills, valleys, lakes, forests, and meadows may be found in the park.

Hampstead Heath provides a variety of outdoor activities in addition to hiking, including swimming in its ponds, playing sports on its sports grounds, and enjoying a picnic. It's a terrific location for families since there are several playgrounds and play spaces for kids. A number of historic sites, including Kenwood House and the Pergola Garden, can be seen in the park, which also has a rich history stretching back to ancient times. Take the Overground rail to Hampstead Heath Station or a bus to one of the several close-by bus stations to get to Hampstead Heath.

Cycling in the Parks: Many of London's parks have designated bike lanes, and the city is home to a number of greenways and cycling routes. A terrific way to see the city and get some exercise at the same time is to rent a bike.

Londoners love to pedal in the parks, and many of them have bike lanes and dedicated cycling pathways to make riding safer and simpler. Hyde Park, Regent's Park, and Greenwich Park are a few of the parks where people like to bike.

If you don't possess a bicycle, you may simply borrow one from one of the city's numerous bike rental businesses or from one of the Santander Cycle Hire docking stations, which are dispersed all over the place. For individuals who don't want to commit to a full-day rental, the Santander Cycle Hire program provides an economical and practical method to borrow a bike for a short amount of time.

Cycling through the green areas of London's parks is a fantastic way to see the city and get some exercise at the same time. There are many possibilities to explore the city on two wheels, regardless of your cycling experience.

The River Thames is one of London's most recognizable sights, and kayaking is a terrific opportunity to see it from a different angle. Kayaking trips are available from a number of businesses, and they are a pleasant and laid-back way to experience the city from the water.

Using a kayak to explore London on the River Thames may be exciting and different. Numerous businesses provide guided kayaking trips, and they often come with all the required gear and training for people who have never paddled before. You'll pass by some of London's most well-known attractions on the journey, including Tower Bridge, the Tower of London, and the London Eye.

Kayaking on the Thames: Kayaking on the Thames is a fantastic way to get some exercise and enjoy the outdoors in addition to taking in the views. It's a fun way to spend a few hours away from the city's bustle and is a reasonably simple pastime that individuals of all ages and fitness levels can enjoy.

In order to guarantee availability, particularly during the high season, it is advised to reserve your trip in advance if you're interested in kayaking on the Thames. Depending on the operator and the season, the excursions may cost anywhere between £30 and £60 and run between 2 and 3 hours.

Rock Climbing in Battersea: The Battersea Park Climbing Wall is a fantastic location for rock climbing and bouldering in Battersea. It's a terrific spot to test your talents and work out since it includes a range of routes for climbers of all experience levels.

One of London's biggest and most beautiful parks, Battersea Park is home to the Battersea Park Climbing Wall. The wall is staffed with knowledgeable and welcoming instructors who provide equipment, such as helmets and harnesses, as well as coaching for novices. It is appropriate for climbers of all skill levels, from novices to experienced climbers, since there are several climbing routes of varied difficulties. You may reserve sessions in advance, and the wall is open every day of the week. Battersea Park provides a wide range of outdoor sports in addition to rock climbing, including tennis, basketball, and boating on the lake. A trip to the Battersea Park Climbing Wall is certainly something you should think about if you're seeking an interesting outdoor activity to do while touring London.

Zip Lining in Greenwich: The Emirates Air Line is a cable vehicle that crosses the Thames between the Royal Docks and the Greenwich Peninsula. It's a fun and interesting outdoor activity and a terrific opportunity to gain a bird's eye perspective of the city.

The Emirates Air Line is not only a useful means to go from one side of the river to the other, but it is also a fun and thrilling way to explore the city. It is a fantastic way to get a feel of the size of the city and provides expansive views of the Thames and the neighborhood. There are stops at both the Royal Docks and in Greenwich, and the trip takes around 10 minutes each way. You may tour the neighborhood, go to museums, or take a stroll in the park when you cross over. The cable car is available year-round, weather permitting, and is accessible to those with impairments. Tickets for the Emirates Air Line may be bought at either station or online, and there are special fares for children, the elderly, and students.

Day Trips From London

CHAPTER 8: DAY TRIPS FROM

LONDON

Ideas for excursions outside of the city

Here are the top excursions from London that we're currently organizing, whether you're looking for a beach getaway or a rural escape.

Even while the city is beautiful in the summer, with 9 million Londoners rushing to the next beer garden, park, or rooftop pub, you could sometimes feel a little claustrophobic as a result of the sheer number of people there.

Thankfully, domestic travel has started to become more accessible this year, with day excursions and overnight stays at hotels, campgrounds, and Airbnb. And when the Big Smoke becomes too much, we can once again go to the ocean, stroll through the forest, or discover a picture-perfect hamlet.

Considering a little vacation? Here are some ideas to help you with your own daydreams. These are 15 of our favorite day-trip destinations, all within a day's drive of London and replete with adorable pubs and fantastic eateries.

15 wonderful day Trips from London

1. The New Forest

The closest thing to going on safari without purchasing a plane ticket is a trip to the New Forest. You will pass by the famed ponies, which have grazed there for thousands of years, as well as free-ranging Highland cattle and pigs scavenging for fallen acorns, as you go through shaded alleys and over the heather-covered heath. Don't want to spend the whole day inside the car? For exploration, rent a two-person Twizzy electric buggy, or reserve a beginner's hack at a nearby stable. Don't forget to set aside time for a traditional plowman's lunch at the Fritham Royal Oak.

How far? 90 miles

Get there Brockenhurst is about a two-hour drive from Waterloo by automobile and one hour and thirty minutes by rail. Just keep in mind that here, animals have the right of way, not drivers.

2. Deal

Deal checks all the boxes for a day trip with its charming rows of Georgian homes, distinctive stores, and beloved Saturday market, even if it may not receive as much attention as Margate and Whitstable do. Treat yourself to lunch at 81 Beach Street or Victuals & Co. after paying a visit to Deal Castle, which Henry VIII built as the first of a magnificent series of coastal forts. Deal Castle was created as the first of a grand series of coastal forts. Delilah the sheepdog will welcome you with open paws at Taylor-Jones & Son, a gallery and home goods store. Stock up on gluggable delights at the Parisian-style bottle store Le Pinardier, and while you're there, don't miss Le Pinardier.

How far? Just over 80 miles

Getting there From St. Pancras International takes one and a half hours by rail and around two hours by vehicle.

3. <u>Box Hill</u>

It's a wheely great way to spend a Sunday riding a bike to Surrey, which is green and beautiful, and Box Hill was on the Olympic road cycling route in 2012. It should take you roughly two hours to ride from Richmond Park past Hampton Court. You'll be rewarded with breathtaking views of the North Downs from Box Hill's summit after a 1.6-mile climb and a few hairpin curves (which are simpler than they seem!). Save room for lunch at The Tree, which offers handmade pies and crumbles, and pick up a piece of cake from the National Trust café. The penultimate stop is Box Hill and Westhumble Station, where you may board a train back to Waterloo with your bicycles in tow. Whew!

How far? 30 miles

Getting there: 2 hours on a bicycle (obviously). Before you go, carefully plan your itinerary; include a map, a puncture repair kit, water, and food.

4. <u>Dungeness</u>

The shingly, shipwreck-dotted beach at Dungeness has been compared to Britain's sole desert because it is so eerily desolate (though the Met Office refuses to technically recognize it as such, the party-poopers). But if you look closely, you can see a lot happening. One reason is that it is a natural reserve. For an opportunity to see glossy ibises and marsh harriers, walk the two-mile loop around RSPB Dungeness. Wait in line at the renowned Dungeness Snack Shack around noon for their catch of the day served in a toasty bun along with lobster and crab rolls or smoked fish soup. Finally, look for the enormous concrete "sound reflectors," which were constructed during World War I and used to detect aircraft.

How far? 86 miles

Getting there: St Pancras International to Folkstone takes one hour by rail, followed by a one-hour, thirty-minute bus journey to Dungeness; the trip takes around two hours by car.

5. <u>Hastings</u>

Hastings has a long and colorful history, from its importance as the site of William the Conqueror's triumph in 1066 to its prominence as a smuggling hub in the eighteenth century. Therefore, it is very understandable why Londoners seeking sun have been flocking to this town for ages like seagulls.

Explore the stunning remains of the town's Norman castle to learn more about its fascinating past, or pay a visit to Smugglers Adventure, a museum located in ancient smugglers' caverns. The Hill Cliff Railway, Britain's steepest funicular, is the perfect place to spend some time admiring the vistas while perusing the unique stores in charming Old Town and strolling along the pier.

How far? 54 miles

Get there From London Bridge, it takes one hour and thirty minutes by rail; two hours by automobile.

6. <u>Mersea Island</u>

Mersea, which is connected to the mainland by a prone-to-flooding bridge, seems really lonely during high tide. Pub quizzers, take note: this is the most easterly inhabited island in the UK. Every weekend, visitors come from all across the country to The Company Shed, which serves seafood platters. Bring your own bread, and reservations are not accepted, so arrive before noon to ensure you can chow down on prawns, smoked salmon, oysters, and dressed crab. Catch-and-release crab fishing is encouraged; there are spots along the water that have been properly designated for it as well as stores that offer the equipment. Or you may reserve a boat tour of the bay.

How far? 69 miles

Get there Two hours by car, one hour by rail from Liverpool Street to Colchester, followed by a 45-minute bus ride to Mersea Island Before you go, make sure to verify the tidal schedule.

7. <u>Whitstable</u>

Whitstable is one of the most charming beach towns I can imagine. There, at Blueprint Coffee and Books, start the day with a pot of coffee robust and responsibly produced (and maybe a mini orange-and-rosemary bundt cake). Next, get a bike from Whitstable Cycle Hire and ride along the five-mile Oyster Bay Trail along the waterfront. also for lunch? Oysters, of course; at The Forge, watch as they are shucked right in front of you. One of the few UK towns with a tavern, the Old Neptune, directly on the shingle is Whitstable. Stay on the beach for a drink while the sun sets.

How far? 61 miles

Get there Whitstable may be reached in one hour and twenty minutes by rail from Victoria or in one hour and ten minutes by vehicle from St. Pancras International.

8. Rye

Rye resembles a little piece of the Cotswolds on the coast thanks to its antique stores and quirky cobblestone pathways. After you've thoroughly perused the aptly called Tiny Book Store, indulge yourself to a seafood meal at Globe Inn Marsh, which is bordered by lobster pots. Then, go to The George Tap for a pint of Sussex genuine ale or a glass of regional wine. If you want to learn about winemaking or just have a drink with their unique wine sampling, the Chapel Down vineyard is nearby and well worth a visit. The pillowy dunes of Camber Sands are just ten minutes away; pull up your pants and splash through the shallows, fly a kite, or simply park your blanket and relax.

How far? 79 miles.

Getting there: approximately two hours by vehicle; one hour and ten minutes by rail (with a change at Ashford) from St. Pancras International.

9. <u>Margate</u>

Margate, a seaside town in Kent, is awash in craft beer and cold-brew coffee, and it has enough seaside charm to stave off blustery sea gusts. Start at the Turner Contemporary art museum before making your way to Dreamland, a vintage theme park, and roller disco. After the waltzer's effects have subsided, visit Hantverk & Found for a meal of fresh fish and organic wines. Shop for exquisite antique goods at Breuer & Dawson and seaweed-based skincare in Haeckels for the remainder of the day.

How far? 76 miles

From St. Pancras International, it takes one hour and 25 minutes to get there by rail; two hours by vehicle.

10. <u>Bath</u>

You're in for a magnificent day with a water theme in Bath. Start out on the right foot by taking a tour of the Roman baths (no swimming, as you have been informed), then make a splash at the Thermae Bath Spa, where the rooftop pool offers great city views. Make like Jane Austen and walk around the Royal Crescent after you've dried off. To really immerse yourself in the past, try on some replica Georgian attire at the Fashion Museum. Peckish? The Sally Lunn Bun, a sweet brioche bap, is a specialty of Sally Lunn's tearoom. For a Bath-style cream tea, request one that has been toasted and covered with strawberry jam and clotted cream.

How far? 115 miles

Come there Train travel from Paddington takes one hour and a half; driving takes two hours and a half.

11. <u>Brighton</u>

Brighton is the best place to top up on Vitamin Sea because of its pebble beach, and an abundance of live music venues. Beginning your day by evading seagulls on the Palace Pier, you can then go shopping to your heart's content in the Lanes, which are brimming with small shops, record stores, and vegan restaurants. Take a seat and enjoy a few beers at the Brighton Beer Dispensary, which supports independent Sussex brewers like the Hand Brew Co.

How far? A little over 50 miles

Come there From Victoria, Blackfriars, or London Bridge, it takes one hour by rail; two hours by automobile.

12. <u>Canterbury</u>

At the time of Chaucer, this was the location of a large religious gathering. Today, Canterbury is a bit more subdued, but there is still a pleasingly raucous edge thanks to the enormous student population. Start out by taking a leisurely walk along the King's Mile, which is lined with stores. You have plenty of options for lunch, like gourmet scotch eggs at Pork & Co with slaw and fries, bento boxes at Tamago, and hot pizza at the indoor farmers' market The Goods Shed. Visit the Beaney House of Art and Knowledge, which has one of the most significant collections of cow paintings in the world and a mummified Egyptian cat, to round off your very own Canterbury story.

How far? 61 miles

Getting there: One hour by rail from St Pancras International; about one hour and thirty minutes by car.

13. <u>Guildford</u>

Attention, aficionados of the macabre: The Guildford Cathedral is the star of the cult classic "The Omen." Despite this, the whole county town of Surrey is quite bucolic. If the weather is nice, you can lay by the sea at charming Dapdune Wharf or even swim in it at the Guildford Lido. Burrito Loco offers nacho boxes made with locally sourced ingredients for lunch. Afterward, visit the 400-year-old Star Inn. Yet thirsty? Take a train to the adjacent Hogs Back Brewery and explore it.

How far? 31 miles

From Waterloo, get there by rail in 30 minutes or by vehicle in around an hour.

14. <u>Southend-on-Sea</u>

There are much worse places to have nostalgic seaside fun than Southend. The area features all the hallmarks of a traditional seaside resort, including amusement parks, carnival attractions, the world's longest pier (which has a railway running down it), old-school chippies, and retro ice-cream parlor Tomassi's. Additionally, it has several ambitious restaurants, such as the fine-dining spot Aurum and the gastropub The Pipe of Port, as well as a developing arts community led by the Focal Point Gallery and the yearly Village Green music and arts festival.

How far? 36 miles

Come there Two hours by vehicle and one hour and fifteen minutes by rail from Fenchurch Street.

15. Cambridge

There is much to keep you engaged at Cambridge, which is more sedate, smaller, and—shudder—prettier than Oxford. Start your vacation off right with a trip to the Fitzwilliam Museum and a meal at Fitzbillies. To take home, be sure to get a package of the sticky Chelsea buns. Spend a couple of hours seeing the colleges and King's Chapel before trying your hand at punting on the river; behatted guides will do the job for you, or you can rent a boat of your own (be warned: it's more difficult than it appears). When it's time for tea, make your way to Grantchester and have scones in The Orchard Tea Gardens as poet Rupert Brooke did.

How far? 64 miles

From King's Cross, it takes 45 minutes to get there by rail, 1 hour 10 from Liverpool Street, and 2 hours or so by automobile.

Tips for planning a day trip from London

Consider taking a day trip from London if you want a break from the rush and bustle of city life. Here are some suggestions for organizing your trip:

Choose your destination: Think about your interests, whether they be in history, culture, outdoor pursuits, or anything else. Stonehenge, Bath, Oxford, and Windsor are a few well-liked day trip locations from London.

Plan your transportation: You may take a train, bus, or a vehicle from London to a lot of locations. Consider the time, cost, and simplicity of travel while deciding on the best route to take to your desired location.

Schedule your trip: Be careful to include in any entry hours or tour schedules for the locations you wish to see when organizing your day excursion. You should also include ample time for meals, other activities, and travel.

Pack appropriately: You may need to pack certain goods, such as sunscreen, a hat, or a picnic meal, depending on your trip. Verify the weather prediction and prepare appropriately.

Pack a picnic: A picnic is an excellent idea to carry with you since many of the locations outside of London are in remote places with few food alternatives. This may help you save money while allowing you to eat in a beautiful atmosphere.

Check the weather: Because England's weather may be erratic, make careful to consult the forecast before making travel arrangements. You may want to think about going somewhere with indoor activities if it's going to rain, like a museum or art gallery.

Allow for flexibility: Having a plan is usually a good idea, but it's also crucial to be adaptable and receptive to surprising findings. Be open to new experiences and try not to adhere to your timetable too strictly since often the highlights of a vacation are the unexpected ones.

Family-Friendly Activities In London

CHAPTER 9: FAMILY-FRIENDLY

ACTIVITIES IN LONDON

Recommendations for things to do with kids in the city

Kids may find a ton of fun and instructive activities in London. There are activities for kids of all interests in this thriving city, whether they are interested in science, history, art, or just having fun. London is a fantastic vacation spot for families since it has top-notch museums and exciting activities. In this article, we'll showcase some of the top family-friendly activities in London, including both well-known attractions and undiscovered secrets. You may discover lots of activities to keep your kids occupied and amused whether you're organizing a day trip or a full-fledged family vacation.

Here are some suggestions for family-friendly activities in London:

- **London Eye:** This enormous Ferris wheel provides amazing city vistas and is a wonderful way to introduce youngsters to London's attractions.

Families visiting the city with children must check out the London Eye. It is 135 meters tall and provides 360-degree views of the city, giving visitors a distinctive vantage point of some of London's most well-known sights, including the River Thames, Buckingham Palace, as well as the Houses of Parliament.

Families may ride the London Eye in comfort and safety thanks to the large, completely enclosed capsules. The 30-minute cruise gives you enough time to take in the sights and soak in the scenery.

Booking your tickets in advance is a fantastic idea since the attraction might become crowded during popular seasons. On the day of your visit, you may buy tickets at the ticket office or online. Standard tickets, fast-track tickets, and champagne experiences are just a few of the many ticket choices that are offered.

A short distance between the London Eye Pier and the London Dungeon, the London Eye is situated on the South Bank of the River Thames, next to the Jubilee Gardens. Waterloo, which is close by and well-linked to other areas of the city, is the closest underground station.

Children will have a great time on the London Eye while learning about the city's history and famous sites. Whether you're a resident or a guest, you won't want to miss this event.

- **Science Museum:** Children who like science and technology will enjoy the hands-on exhibits at the Science Museum. It is a fun location to spend a few hours since it has a range of interactive exhibits and performances.

One of London's top attractions for families and children is the Science Museum. It is situated in South Kensington and provides kids with an entertaining method to learn about science and technology. The museum includes more than 15,000 items on view, including a sizable collection of old scientific equipment, interactive exhibitions, and live demonstrations.

The Wonderlab, a hands-on section where children may learn science via interactive displays and activities, is one of the attractions of the museum. Children may explore interactive exhibits in this section to learn about electricity, light, and sound, and they can even try their hand at designing their own experiments.

The Science Museum's IMAX theater, which screens a range of educational and science-related movies, is another well-liked attraction. The museum also hosts a variety of temporary exhibits, which are often devoted to certain branches of technology or science, including robots or space exploration.

All visitors are welcome at the Science Museum, which is open every day from 10:00 a.m. to 6:00 p.m. The closest tube station is South Kensington, making it simple to get to the museum via public transit. For families and children visiting London, the Science Museum is a must-visit location because of its interesting exhibits and interactive displays.

- **Buckingham Palace:** Kids who are interested in history and monarchy must visit Buckingham Palace. They may witness the palace's lovely grounds and the ceremony of the Changing of the Guard.

One of London's most recognizable sights, Buckingham Palace serves as the official home of the British queen. It is conveniently close to public transit and situated in the center of the city. During the summer, the palace is available to the public, who may explore the state rooms and see the fine artwork, furniture, and decorations on show.

The Changing of the Guard ceremony, which happens every day at 11:30 a.m. at Buckingham Palace, is one of the most well-liked activities for children there. Kids will enjoy seeing the troops in their full uniforms, including their crimson coats and black bearskin helmets, during this customary military ritual when the palace guard is replaced.

Visitors may tour the palace's lovely grounds, the biggest private gardens in London, and a tranquil haven in the middle of the bustling metropolis, in addition to the palace itself. There are lots of walks and lawns for youngsters to run about on, and the gardens are home to a variety of animals, including ducks, squirrels, and birds.

For children of all ages, going to Buckingham Palace is a terrific opportunity to learn about the history and culture of London and is also a ton of fun. It is advised that you get your tickets in advance and come to the palace early to beat the crowds in order to have a smooth and pleasurable experience.

- **Sea Life London:** Sharks, rays, and sea turtles are just a few of the thousands of marine animals that call this aquarium home. While watching them swim in their tanks, children may learn about the many varieties.

For families with children interested in marine life, Sea Life London is a must-visit location. The aquarium, which is centrally located in the city, gives visitors of all ages an engaging and instructive experience. With more than 600 kinds of marine life, including sharks, rays, seahorses, and sea turtles, tourists may discover the variety of marine life that lives in our waters.

One of the aquarium's features is the Ocean Tube, a 360-degree walk-through tunnel where guests can get close to aquatic life, including enormous green sea turtles and blacktip reef sharks. The Rock Pool, where children may interact with and learn about starfish, sea urchins, and other species, is another well-liked destination.

The aquarium also has a number of interactive displays, such as the Interactive Rockpool, where children can discover more about the species that live in the rock pool and even get up close to some of them. The Penguins Rock exhibit is also a must-see since it gives guests a close-up view of the amusing penguins and teaches them about their habitats and behavior.

At County Hall, Westminster Bridge Road, London, SE1 7PB, the United Kingdom, you can find Sea Life London. Callers may reach them at +44 20 7967 8000. Check their website for the most recent details since admission costs sometimes change.

Water Life London is a fantastic option whether you're searching for a family-friendly day out or just want to learn more about the fascinating world of sea animals.

Harry Potter Studio Tour: Your youngsters will enjoy seeing the filming location if they are fans of the Harry Potter novels and movies. They may see the backdrops, furnishings, and attire while learning about cinematic magic.

Any fan of the Harry Potter universe must take the Harry Potter Studio Tour. The studio tour, which is situated in Leavesden not far from London by rail, provides guests with an up-close and personal view of the production of the Harry Potter movies.

With intricate sets, costumes, and accessories on display, visitors are immediately immersed in the wonderful world of Harry Potter upon entering the studio. You may stroll through Diagon Alley, see Hagrid's hut, tour the Great Hall, and view the Gryffindor common room.

The chance to see the usage of special effects in the movies, from the development of characters like Dobby the house elf to the flying scenes on broomsticks, is one of the tour's highlights. Additionally, there is a showcase of storyboards and concept drawings, which helps visitors have a better knowledge of the filmmaking process.

Along with the tour, there is a café and a gift store where you can have a Butterbeer or pick up something to take home as a memento of your trip. It is advised to purchase your tour tickets in advance to avoid standing in line and waiting.

Fans of the series will be delighted by the Harry Potter Studio Tour, which is a memorable experience for both children and adults. So be ready to enjoy the enchantment of the Harry Potter movies and bring your wand!

- **London Zoo:** The London Zoo, which can be found in Regent's Park, is home to over 700 different types of animals, including flamingos, lions, and gorillas. It's a fantastic location to learn about wildlife and interact closely with some of the most intriguing species on the planet.

One of the most well-liked family-friendly attractions in the city is the London Zoo, which provides a variety of experiences and activities for children of all ages. The zoo includes interactive displays, animal feedings, and chances for youngsters to engage directly with some of the animals, such as the petting zoo, in addition to the chance to observe and learn about a range of species.

Visitors may also tour the zoo's different habitats, such as the Gorilla Kingdom, Penguin Beach, and Rainforest Life exhibits, each of which gives a distinctive perspective on the animals and their surroundings.

The Zoo Lates events, which are reserved for adults and take place after the zoo has closed to the general public, are among the most well-liked attractions at the London Zoo. These gatherings provide the chance to visit the zoo after hours, as well as live music, food, and beverages.

A number of bus and metro lines that stop at the neighboring Camden Town station provide easy access to the London Zoo, which is open every day save Christmas Day. Tickets may be bought in advance or on the day of the visit, and there are discounts for kids, students, and seniors.

- **The Natural History Museum:** The South Kensington location of this famous museum offers a broad range of interactive displays, such as a life-size blue whale skeleton, a butterfly exhibit, and a sizable fossil collection.

Families with kids like visiting the Natural History Museum because it has so many engaging displays and educational opportunities. The museum's vast collections of fossils, minerals, and living creatures, including one of its most recognizable exhibits—a life-size blue whale skeleton—can be explored by visitors.

The interactive displays at the museum are intended to excite and motivate young minds and provide kids with a fun, hands-on method to learn about nature. Visitors may see real butterflies from all over the globe in the museum's butterfly display, for instance, and can get a close-up view of dinosaurs and ammonites in the fossil collections.

The Natural History Museum provides a range of temporary exhibits in addition to its permanent collections, as well as family-friendly educational activities and programs. On-site, there is a museum store that sells a variety of trinkets, educational toys, and books.

Since the Natural History Museum is free to enter, it is a convenient and reasonably priced activity for families traveling to London. The museum is open every day from 10:00 am to 5:30 pm and is conveniently located near a variety of public transit options. South Kensington is the closest subway station, and a number of bus lines also pass by the museum.

The Tower of London: One of the city's most famous sites, the Tower of London is interesting for families to visit. You may take a tour of the castle, see the Crown Jewels, and discover more about the intriguing structure's past.

Over the course of its 900-year existence, the Tower of London has functioned as a palace, a jail, and a location for executions. It now ranks among the most well-liked tourist destinations in London and provides a variety of thrilling experiences for tourists of all ages.

The Crown Jewels, which are kept in the Jewel House and include some of the most priceless and spectacular diamonds, emeralds, and rubies in the world, are one of the Tower of London's most well-known attractions. The several towers of the castle, such as the White Tower, where children can see medieval armor and weaponry, and the Bloody Tower, where they can discover information about some of the renowned inmates who were housed there, will also be enjoyed by children.

The Tower of London provides a variety of activities and events geared exclusively at families in addition to the tours and exhibits. Visitors may, for instance, take a Yeoman Warder tour to learn about the castle's history and notable inmates, or they can take part in a practical workshop to put on medieval armor or create a crown.

The Tower of London is open from Tuesday through Saturday from 9:00 am to 5:00 pm and on Sundays and bank holidays from 10:00 am to 5:00 pm. It is situated at St Katherine's & Wapping, London, EC3N 4AB. Adults must pay admission; however, children under 16 may enter free of charge.

In London, there are many entertaining and instructive activities for youngsters. There are lots for youngsters of all ages to enjoy, from the Natural History Museum and the Tower of London to the many parks and open areas. In this dynamic and interesting city, there are several possibilities to make special memories with your family, regardless of your interests in history, science, or the outdoors. So, if you're considering taking your kids on a vacation to London, make sure to take into account these well-liked attractions and activities. You'll create lifelong memories and your kids will undoubtedly have fun.

Tips for planning a family-friendly trip to London

With a vast range of sights and activities suited for children of all ages, London is a fantastic vacation spot for families. Here are some suggestions for organizing a city vacation that's suitable for families:

Choose the right accommodation: Think about booking a room at a hotel or apartment that welcomes families and has adequate space for everyone. Think about the area as well; for families with small children, staying close to a park or other green area might be a terrific choice.

When selecting a place to stay, it's crucial to take your family's requirements into account. Selecting a location with a kitchenette may be beneficial for families with small children so that you may make meals or snacks. To make your stay more pleasant, many London hotels and flats also provide cribs, high chairs, and other baby equipment.

Selecting the ideal lodging requires careful consideration of location. Staying close to a park or other open area may be a terrific way to get away from the bustle of the city and give chances for play and outdoor activities. Being near public transit may also make it simpler to navigate the city and reach London's numerous family-friendly attractions.

Your preferred kind of lodging is a further factor: You could choose a serviced apartment or a vacation rental if you want to feel more at home, while a family-friendly hotel with features like a kids' club or a pool can be more convenient. Regardless of the kind of lodging you choose, be sure to read reviews and inquire about family-friendly choices before making a reservation.

Plan your itinerary in advance: Make a strategy to guarantee that everyone gets to experience the things they are interested in by deciding what you want to see and do as a family.

When making your itinerary, it's a good idea to take the time of day and the quantity of walking into account. When you have small children, it's usually preferable to plan more leisurely activities first, like museum trips, and save the more physically demanding ones, like a lengthy stroll in the park, for later in the day. In order to give everyone a chance to unwind and recharge, it's a good idea to schedule some leisure, such as a picnic in the park or a trip to a nearby playground.

Accessibility is a crucial factor to take into account while organizing a family-friendly vacation to London. Be careful to choose family-friendly activities and attractions, taking into consideration any physical restrictions or mobility concerns. Visitors with disabilities may access several well-known tourist attractions in London, and there are many services available to assist you in organizing an accessible vacation.

It's a good idea to do some advanced study on activity costs so you can adjust your budget properly. Take advantage of the family discounts that many of London's biggest sites, like the London Eye and the Tower of London, offer whenever you can. You can make sure that everyone has a good time, has a memorable experience, and enjoys themselves on your family-friendly vacation to London by preparing ahead and being considerate of everyone's needs and interests.

Take advantage of free attractions: Families will love London's numerous free attractions, which include parks and museums. To save expenditures, think about going to the Science Museum, National Gallery, or British Museum.

It's a smart idea to take advantage of the city's many free attractions while organizing a family-friendly vacation to London. The entire family may have a fun and instructive experience at these sites while also reducing expenditures.

One of London's most famous free attractions, the British Museum is a terrific spot to spend the day with the kids. The museum is the place where a sizable collection of items from all around the globe, such as the Parthenon sculptures and the Rosetta Stone, are kept. It's a terrific method to expose youngsters to history and culture since it has many hands-on exhibitions and interactive displays.

The National Gallery, which has a sizable collection of European paintings from the 13th to the 19th centuries, is another fantastic free destination. There is art here for everyone, whether you are interested in Impressionist or Renaissance classics. The National Gallery is a terrific site to visit with children because of its family-friendly activities and workshops as well as its kid-friendly audio tour.

Another excellent choice for families is the Science Museum, which offers engaging displays and practical activities that will keep youngsters occupied for several hours. The Science Museum has something for everyone, from the evolution of technology to the history of space flight.

In addition to these museums, London has a ton of additional cost-free family-friendly activities including parks and gardens, public art projects, and historic sites. You may discover a ton of entertaining and instructive activities that are ideal for your family's vacation to London if you do a little research.

Make use of public transportation: Buses, trains, and the Underground are all part of London's huge public transit system, which makes getting about the city with kids simple. Get an Oyster Card to travel quickly and easily.

London's public transit system may make getting about the city with kids simple and effective. All types of public transit in London, including buses, trains, and the Underground, accept Oyster Cards as payment. Given that you may take as many journeys as you like within a certain time frame and that there are fee savings available, it is a practical and economical method of transportation.

When traveling with children, it's crucial to make sure they are seated safely and securely on buses, trains, and the Underground, and that they are always under adult supervision. The distance between the station and your destination, as well as any stairs or escalators that must be taken, should all be taken into account when planning your route in advance.

In addition to using public transit, you may want to think about taking a cab or utilizing a ride-hailing service like Uber since these options can be more practical and pleasant for families. To select the ideal solution for your requirements, it's crucial to investigate the possibilities and compare pricing and services.

Plan for meals and snacks: In London, eating out might be pricey, so think about packing snacks and beverages with you. If you do decide to dine out, seek eateries with kid-friendly menus or family-friendly choices.

It's a good idea to schedule your meals in advance and search for family-friendly places. It's important doing some research ahead of time to identify the best possibilities as many restaurants offer special specials or discounts for youngsters. You may also think about going to more informal restaurants like cafés or food markets, which often offer more economical selections and a more laid-back ambiance. For added convenience in case your kids feel hungry in between meals, think about packing a portable water bottle as well as some snacks, such as fruit or granola bars. This may both save you money and keep your family well-fed and active throughout the day.

Consider a family-friendly tour: A guided tour may be a fantastic opportunity for your family to explore the attractions and learn about the city. Look for family-friendly excursions, or hire a private guide to create an itinerary just for you.

Consider taking a guided tour while organizing a family-friendly vacation to London. Making the most of your time in the city and ensuring that your family has the opportunity to see all of the sites and attractions that are most pertinent to your interests and requirements may be accomplished in this manner.

There are many various kinds of trips available, from big-group excursions to private, individualized excursions designed just for your family's interests. You could think about hiring a private guide for a more in-depth experience since they can build an itinerary, especially for your family, and can provide more individualized care.

Make sure to take your children's age and interests into account while choosing a trip, as well as your personal preferences. For instance, you may choose a walking tour to show you around some of the most charming and historic parts of the city or a culinary tour to let you experience some of London's delectable cuisine.

Booking a trip that is suitable for families and kids is an excellent alternative. These tours often include enjoyable, engaging activities like treasure hunts, scavenger hunts, and hands-on workshops that are intended to keep youngsters interested and delighted.

A guided tour is a fantastic way to make the most of your family's time in London and make sure that everyone has a special and pleasurable experience, regardless of the style of trip you choose.

You can make sure your family has a delightful and unforgettable vacation to London by keeping these suggestions in mind.

Planning Your Trip To London

CHAPTER 10: PLANNING YOUR TRIP

TO LONDON

Tips for booking flights and accommodation

Booking flights and lodging might be difficult when organizing a vacation to London, but it can also be an exhilarating experience. With so many choices, it's crucial to be certain of your spending limit, departure date, and preferences.

There are a few suggestions to bear in mind while making travel arrangements for a family vacation to London in order to obtain the greatest value for your money:

Book in advance: Advance reservations may help you obtain the greatest deals and provide you with a larger selection of possibilities. This is especially true for flights and lodging.

Making reservations in advance might also make it easier for you to arrange your calendar and activities around your trip dates. Families who are on a trip with small children may find this to be particularly crucial since they may have particular requirements and timetables. By making your reservations in advance, you can guarantee that your accommodations will fit your requirements and that you will have enough time to organize your activities and make any required preparations.

Compare prices: Comparing costs Utilize internet travel services to evaluate costs and discover the finest offers on lodging and flights. Keep an eye out for any specials and unique offers that may be offered, such as early bird discounts or package packages.

It's crucial to check costs from many websites while looking for flights and lodging to ensure you're getting the greatest bargain. A practical method to accomplish this is via online travel services, which let you rapidly compare costs and amenities from several airlines, inns, and other lodging options.

When utilizing these websites, make sure to keep an eye out for any specials and unique bargains that could be available, such as early bird discounts, package discounts, and incentives from loyalty programs. To determine whether they provide better pricing, you could also wish to take into account other airports, such as neighboring regional airports.

Check the airlines' and hotels' own websites as well since they can have deals or promotions that aren't offered on other travel websites. To make your vacation more pleasant and convenient if you're traveling with kids, seek family-friendly lodging options, such as hotels with kids' clubs or flats with kitchens.

Before making a reservation, be sure to thoroughly read the terms and conditions. If you have any concerns, don't hesitant to ask them. This will make sure that your time in London goes well and that you enjoy yourself.

You may use the following well-known travel sites to compare costs for lodging and flights in London:

- Expedia: https://www.expedia.com/
- Booking.com: https://www.booking.com/
- Hotels.com: https://www.hotels.com/
- Kayak: https://www.kayak.com/
- Orbitz: https://www.orbitz.com/
- Priceline: https://www.priceline.com/
- Travelocity: https://www.travelocity.com/
- TripAdvisor: https://www.tripadvisor.com/

You may compare airfare, hotel, and other lodging costs on these websites, as well as read reviews from other travelers. You may get the most affordable lodging and airfare for your family-friendly vacation to London by utilizing these websites.

Travel during low season: Consider going during the low season, when costs are cheaper and crowds are less, if at all feasible. This may be a fantastic method to save costs while improving the quality of your vacation.

There are several benefits to traveling off-peak, including cheaper rates and less congestion. In London, the low season normally lasts from November to February, when the weather is colder and there are fewer visitors. If you want to escape the peak-season crowds and save money on flights and lodging, this might be a terrific time to go. You could also discover that at this time, places of interest and museums are less crowded, making it simpler to see and do all you desire. You may be able to save money on meals and shopping since many restaurants and stores run special specials and bargains to entice visitors during the slow season. You may have a more leisurely and pleasurable vacation without going over budget if you go during the low season.

The low season in London is often seen as occurring from January through February and from November through December when the temperature is colder and there are fewer visitors. If you want to go when there are fewer people around and the costs are lower, this could be a nice time to go. Remember that during this period, several well-known tourist sites can have shortened hours or be closed for upkeep.

Choose family-friendly accommodations: Look for family-friendly accommodations when making your hotel reservations, such as family-friendly flats or motels. By doing this, you can be sure that your family will have enough room and the necessary conveniences.

Family-friendly lodgings often have bigger rooms or suites that may house more guests as well as perhaps having separate bedrooms for parents and kids. Additionally, they could offer kitchenettes, in-room entertainment, or on-site amenities like playgrounds or swimming pools. Another crucial factor to take into account while selecting family-friendly lodging is its location. To make it easier to go back and forth from your hotel, look for lodging that is near landmarks, parks, and other family-friendly activities. Consider staying at a hotel that serves breakfast or other meals since this may save you time and money, particularly if you have small children. Last but not least, check out reviews from other families to learn what they liked and disliked about the lodging, then choose a hotel that fits your family's requirements and price range.

Be adaptable: You may be able to locate better offers on flights and lodging if you're willing to change your vacation dates or your itinerary. Be ready to adapt your plans if required, so be flexible.

Being adaptable gives you the chance to benefit from last-minute offers or off-peak rates, which may help you save money on your vacation. For instance, you may be able to discover cheaper rates on flights and lodging if you're willing to go during the week rather than on the weekends. Additionally, you may be able to save money and get a fresh perspective on the city if you're willing to stay in a different area or use alternate modes of transportation, including public transit or bike rentals. It's vital to have a basic concept of what you want to do and see when organizing your vacation, but being flexible may help you save money and make the most of your family-friendly trip to London.

Finally, think about getting travel insurance to safeguard your family from unforeseen occurrences like airline delays, medical problems, or lost or stolen property. This might give you peace of mind and make you feel assured and ready for your journey.

Families going to London or anywhere else may find that investing in travel insurance is a wise decision. Travel insurance may provide extra advantages like 24-hour help, travel aid services, and emergency evacuation coverage in addition to providing coverage for unanticipated occurrences like airline cancellations, medical problems, or lost or stolen things. Make sure you properly read the policy and comprehend what is and is not covered before obtaining travel insurance. In order to protect yourself in case you need to modify or cancel your plans, it's crucial to buy a policy that offers sufficient coverage for your requirements and budget as soon as you book your trip. You may feel secure, prepared, and at ease when traveling if you get travel insurance since you and your family will be covered in the event of any unforeseen circumstances.

You may compare and buy travel insurance from a variety of internet sites.

Some well-known companies that provide travel insurance are:

- World Nomads
- Allianz Global Assistance
- Travel Guard
- InsureMyTrip
- Squaremouth

To locate the best travel insurance for your family's requirements, evaluate the plans, coverage, and costs offered by various companies. Review the policy terms thoroughly to ensure that you are aware of any exclusions or limits, as well as what is and isn't covered. Read customer testimonials and ratings to get a sense of the quality of each provider's assistance and customer service.

These suggestions will help you plan a pleasant, convenient, and fun vacation to London with your family by helping you identify the finest flights and lodging options.

Suggestions for budgeting and saving money during your trip

Making a budget and conserving money while traveling are essential components of organizing a successful and pleasurable vacation to London. With so many incredible views, experiences, and activities available, it's critical to ensure that you're getting the most for your money. There are several methods to stick to a budget and save money in London, whether you're traveling with your family, as a couple, or by yourself. This guide will assist you in making the most of your money and experiencing everything that London has to offer, from finding the greatest discounts on travel and lodging to dining and shopping like a native. So let's get started and investigate all the many methods you may budget and save money while visiting London.

Here are some ideas for sticking to a spending plan and saving money when visiting London:

- **Research the cost of living:** Research the cost of living in London, including the price of food, transportation, and activities, before you go. By doing this, you may make a budget and make sure you have enough cash on hand to meet your living costs while you're away.

- **Stay in budget-friendly accommodation:** Take into account booking a stay at a hostel, an Airbnb, or a low-cost hotel. This may be an excellent method to save costs while still getting a cozy place to stay.

- **Take advantage of free activities:** In London, there are plenty of attractions to see and things to do that are free, such as visiting parks, museums, and historical sites. To take advantage of these free possibilities, do some research and plan your schedule.

- **Eat like a local:** One of the most expensive aspects of any vacation is eating out. To save money, think about dining like a native by tasting street food or preparing your own meals.

- **Take public transportation:** In London, it is practical, effective, and reasonably priced. Use the city's bus, rail, and subterranean transportation by purchasing an Oyster card or other travel card.

- **Walk or bike:** Walking or bicycling is a convenient, economical, and environmentally responsible way to travel about the city and see the sites. To save money on transportation, think about hiring a bike for the day or doing your exploration on foot.

- **Eat like a local:** Instead of dining out every meal, think about preparing part of your own food or visiting neighborhood markets and food stands. This may be a fantastic way to learn about the local way of life while also saving money.

- **Avoid tourist traps:** These establishments often charge exorbitant prices. To stay away from these regions and choose more affordable choices, do some research and plan your schedule.

- **Use a travel rewards credit card:** If you have a rewards credit card, you may want to use it to cover your London-related expenditures. By doing this, you may accumulate points and miles that you can use for discounts on subsequent travel.

A final checklist of things to do before you go on your trip to London

It is not difficult to see why London is considered to be one of the most popular travel destinations in the whole globe. In this bustling metropolis, there is something for everyone to enjoy thanks to the city's extensive cultural offerings, which include world-class museums and galleries, breathtaking architecture, and a never-ending supply of opportunities for amusement. However, before you start gathering your belongings and making your way to the airport, it is essential to double-check that everything is in order. Creating a comprehensive to-do list of items to do before departing for London may be of great assistance in ensuring that your vacation goes off without a hitch and that you have the most enjoyable experience that is humanly possible. This book will assist you in getting ready for your journey, regardless of whether you will be going on it by yourself, with your family, or with your friends.

Before you leave for your vacation to London, here is one last checklist of items that you need to complete:

- **Confirm your travel itinerary:** Verify your travel itinerary by checking the timings of your flight, train, or bus ride, and ensuring that you have a complete understanding of when you will arrive and when you will leave from your destination.

- **Book your accommodation:** Make sure you have somewhere to stay during your vacation, whether it is a hotel, an Airbnb, or a hostel. This is an important step that should not be overlooked.

- **Purchase travel insurance:** You should seriously consider investing in travel insurance so that you are protected in the event that anything unforeseen occurs, such as a flight being canceled, a medical emergency, or lost or stolen belongings.

- **Make a currency exchange:** If you are departing from a nation other than the United Kingdom, you will be required to make a currency conversion into British pounds.

- **Check for visa requirements:** Depending on where you're coming from, you may need a visa to enter the UK. Make sure you're aware of any visa requirements and have all the necessary documents before you travel.

- **Pack appropriately:** When preparing your suitcase, be sure to include clothes and other things that are suitable for the season you'll be visiting London in as well as the climate there.

- **Make a plan for your activities:** Determine which sights, tours, and activities you want to visit and participate in, and then design your schedule to accommodate those choices.

- Research transportation options: Become familiar with the various modes of transportation available in the city, including public transit, taxis, and walking.

- **Make copies of vital documents:** Before going on your trip, you should make copies of your passport, your travel insurance policy, and any other necessary documents you will need to bring with you.

- **Get your phone ready:** Before you go, double-check that your phone is unlocked and in working order, and think about buying a travel SIM card that you can use in the UK.

You will be able to guarantee that your vacation to London is well-planned, organized, and pleasurable if you complete this checklist in its entirety.

Valuable

Resources

CHAPTER 11: VALUABLE

RESOURCES

Emergency contacts

When planning a trip, it's important to make sure you have the necessary emergency contacts with you. Here are some important contacts you should have on hand while you're in London:

- **Embassy or Consulate of your home country:** This is the first place you should contact if you lose your passport, become a victim of crime, or are in any other kind of emergency.
- Local police: If you need immediate assistance, dial 999.

- **Local hospitals or medical facilities:** Make sure you know where the nearest hospital or medical facility is located, in case of an emergency.

- **Travel insurance provider:** If you have purchased travel insurance, keep the emergency contact information for your provider with you.

- **Family or friends:** Make sure someone back home has your travel itinerary and knows how to reach you in case of an emergency.

- **Hotel or accommodation contact information:** Keep the contact information for your hotel or other accommodation with you at all times.

- **A travel agent or tour operator:** If you have booked a tour or package through a travel agent or tour operator, keep their contact information with you.

The UK's emergency services number is 999, which can be called for police, fire, and ambulance services.

- The Foreign, Commonwealth & Development Office (FCDO) provides consular assistance to British citizens traveling abroad. They can be reached at +44 20 7008 1500.

- The National Health Service (NHS) offers medical assistance to visitors to the UK. If you require medical attention, you should visit an NHS hospital or clinic, or call the non-emergency number 111 for advice.

By having these important contacts with you, you can feel more secure and prepared while you're traveling.

First aid advice for kids

If your child becomes ill or injured while on a trip, it's important to know what steps to take. Here are some tips for providing first aid to children:

- **Prepare a first aid kit:** Before you leave for your trip, make sure you have a first aid kit that is suitable for children. This should include items such as adhesive bandages, antiseptic wipes, pain relief medication, and any other items that you think your child may need.

257

- **Know how to treat common ailments:** Make sure you know how to treat common ailments such as headaches, minor cuts, and insect bites. Keep the appropriate medication and supplies in your first aid kit.

- **Learn CPR:** Knowing CPR can be a life-saving skill, especially for children. Consider taking a CPR course before your trip to ensure that you are prepared in case of an emergency.

- **Find a nearby doctor or hospital:** Before you leave for your trip, research nearby medical facilities and make a note of their location and contact information. In case of an emergency, you should know where to go for medical assistance.

- **Be prepared for emergencies:** Make sure you know what to do in case of an emergency. Make a plan for how you would respond to different types of emergencies and ensure that everyone in your group knows the plan.

Remember, the most important thing you can do is to be prepared and stay calm in an emergency situation. By taking the time to plan ahead and familiarize yourself with first aid procedures, you can help ensure that your trip to London is safe and enjoyable for the whole family.

Medical helplines and pharmacy helplines

In the case of a medical emergency, it's important to have access to medical help quickly. In London, there are a number of medical helplines and pharmacies that can provide assistance.

Here are a few emergency medical helplines that you may find useful:

- **NHS 111:** This is the National Health Service's non-emergency medical helpline. You can call 111 for advice and information on a range of health issues.

- **London Ambulance Service:** In case of a medical emergency, dial 999 to request an ambulance.

- Walk-in Centers: There are several walk-in centers in London where you can receive medical treatment for minor injuries and illnesses.

- **Pharmacies:** Many pharmacies in London offer advice and over-the-counter treatments for a range of health issues. You can find a list of 24-hour pharmacies in London on the NHS website.

It is recommended to carry with you information such as the address and phone number of your hotel or accommodation, your travel insurance policy details, and any important medical information for your family, such as allergies and existing medical conditions. Having these details on hand can be useful in case of an emergency.

In addition to emergency medical helplines, it's also a good idea to know the location of a few local pharmacies in case you need over-the-counter medication or have a minor health concern. Most pharmacies in London are open during normal business hours, and some may have extended hours or be open 24 hours a day. You can find a list of local pharmacies on the NHS website or by using a search engine.

It's important to note that medical care in London can be expensive for those who are not covered by the National Health Service, so it's a good idea to have adequate travel insurance in place.

London Travel

Guide 2023

CONCLUSION

In this book, "London Travel Guide 2023: The Complete London Tourist Guide and Information to make you Experience the city like a true local," we've covered a comprehensive range of topics to help you plan and enjoy your trip to London. We started with a brief overview of the city's history and culture, and then went on to recommend top attractions and activities to experience, including world-famous landmarks, museums, parks, and more. We also provided recommendations for outdoor adventures, family-friendly activities, and things to do for a more cultural experience.

In addition, we offered tips for planning a day trip from London, as well as a family-friendly trip, including advice on flights and accommodations, budgeting and saving money, and important checklists. We also discussed emergency contacts and medical helplines that you may need during your trip. Overall, our goal was to provide you with the information and resources you need to have an enjoyable and memorable trip to London.

We hope that this book has been a valuable resource for you as you plan your trip to London. With all the information and tips provided, you're sure to have a successful and happy journey in the city.

Don't forget to have fun, be open-minded, and make memories that will last a lifetime!

REFERENCES

Waywell, C. (2022, August 7). 17 Best Day Trips From London | Day Trip Ideas Near London. Retrieved February 9, 2023, from Time Out London website: https://www.timeout.com/london/travel/the-best-day-trips-from-london

Norah, L. (2016, August 6). How to Get Around London: A Guide to Public Transport in London - Finding the Universe. Retrieved February 7, 2023, from Finding the Universe website: https://www.findingtheuniverse.com/guide-public-transport-london/

Norah, L. (2016, November 13). Oyster Card vs Contactless: How to Pay for Public Transport in London - Finding the Universe. Retrieved February 7, 2023, from Finding the Universe website: https://www.findingtheuniverse.com/pay-public-transport-london-oyster-contactless-best/

Dodsworth, L. (2014, May 15). Boutique on a budget: Affordable hotels in London. Retrieved February 8, 2023, from On the Luce travel blog website: https://www.ontheluce.com/budget-luxe-accommodation-in-london/

Japhe, B. (2022, April 19). Where To Eat And Drink In London Right Now. *Forbes.* Retrieved from https://www.forbes.com/sites/bradjaphe/2022/04/18/what-to-eat-and-drink-in-london-right-now/?sh=78e67f8c5f52

Vintage Shops in Brick Lane and Shoreditch — London x London. (2022, September 29). Retrieved February 9, 2023, from London x London website: https://www.londonxlondon.com/vintage-shops-brick-lane-shoreditch/

Shopping in London: 14 Best Areas to Shop — London x London. (2022, November 6). Retrieved February 9, 2023, from London x London website: https://www.londonxlondon.com/best-shopping-areas-london/

The 14 Best Museums In London, England | CuddlyNest. (2022, December 13). Retrieved February 9, 2023, from CuddlyNest

Travel Blog | Unique Experiences and Travel Inspiration website: https://www.cuddlynest.com/blog/best-london-museums/

9 of the Best Parks and Green Spaces in London. (2022). Retrieved February 9, 2023, from Wanderlust website: https://www.wanderlust.co.uk/content/best-parks-green-spaces-in-london/

Made in the USA
Las Vegas, NV
21 March 2023